MW01108330

Football

Other titles in the Science Behind Sports series:

Football

JENNIFER GUESS MCKERLEY

LUCENT BOOKS
A part of Gale, Cengage Learning

Detroit • New York • San Francisco • New Haven, Conn • Waterville, Maine • London

LIBRARY OF CONGRESS CATALOGING-IN-PUBLICATION DATA

McKerley, Jennifer Guess.
  Football / by Jennifer Guess Mckerley.
    p. cm. -- (Science behind sports)
  Includes bibliographical references and index.
  ISBN 978-1-4205-0594-8 (hardback)
1. Football--Juvenile literature. 2. Sports sciences--Juvenile literature. I. Title.
  GV950.7.M38 2011
  796.332--dc23

                                                                2011041998

Lucent Books
27500 Drake Rd
Farmington Hills MI 48331

ISBN-13: 978-1-4205-0594-8
ISBN-10: 1-4205-0594-7

Printed in the United States of America

1 2 3 4 5 6 7 16 15 14 13 12

TABLE OF CONTENTS

FOREWORD

On March 21, 1970, Slovenian ski jumper Vinko Bogataj took a terrible fall while competing at the Ski-flying World Championships in Oberstdorf, West Germany. Bogataj's pinwheeling crash was caught on tape by an ABC *Wide World of Sports* film crew and eventually became synonymous with "the agony of defeat" in competitive sporting. While many viewers were transfixed by the severity of Bogataj's accident, most were not aware of the biomechanical and environmental elements behind the skier's fall—heavy snow and wind conditions that made the ramp too fast and Bogataj's inability to maintain his center of gravity and slow himself down. Bogataj's accident illustrates that, no matter how mentally and physically prepared an athlete may be, scientific principles—such as momentum, gravity, friction, and aerodynamics—always have an impact on performance.

Lucent Book's Science Behind Sports series explores these and many more scientific principles behind some of the most popular team and individual sports, including baseball, hockey, gymnastics, wrestling, swimming, and skiing. Each volume in the series focuses on one sport or group of related sports. The volumes open with a brief look at the featured sport's origins, history and changes, then move on to cover the biomechanics and physiology of playing, related health and medical concerns, and the causes and treatment of sports-related injuries.

In addition to learning about the arc behind a curve ball, the impact of centripetal force on a figure skater, or how water buoyancy helps swimmers, Science Behind Sports readers will also learn how exercise, training, warming up, and diet and nutrition directly relate to peak performance and enjoyment of the sport. Volumes may also cover why certain sports are popular, how sports function in the business world, and which hot sporting issues—sports doping and cheating, for example—are in the news.

Basic physical science concepts, such as acceleration, kinetics, torque, and velocity, are explained in an engaging and accessible manner. The full-color text is augmented by fact boxes, sidebars, photos, and detailed diagrams, charts and graphs. In addition, a subject-specific glossary, bibliography and index provide further tools for researching the sports and concepts discussed throughout Science Behind Sports.

CHAPTER 1

The Games Begin

American football had its start in England. For centuries, fans in both countries have told the story about a boy who helped invent the sport. In 1823, William Webb Ellis attended the Rugby School in Great Britain and enjoyed playing a tough game called football. It was like soccer except that a player could catch a kicked ball with his hands, and then he could set the ball down before kicking it in the other direction. Many schools had different sets of rules for this game they called "football." Although the rules were not written down, players knew and understood each school's version of the game. At Rugby it was understood that a player did not carry the ball or run with it.

One written rule did exist at Rugby. The rule stated that when the five o'clock bell rang each afternoon, all sports on campus must end immediately. Students had to stop a game whether it was finished or not. One day the bell chimed just as William caught a long kick. He did not have time to score a goal by kicking the ball into play again, so he quickly decided to try something different. Tucking his head down, he ran and carried the ball through the other players all the way to the goal line. The opposing team members stood shocked. Some said they thought he was stealing the ball to keep for himself. William touched the ball down across the goal line to score just before the final ring of the bell. Then there was a big argument about whether his play should count or not.

Game Change

It is not known what the players decided about William's spontaneous action. It is a popular belief that he made the first touchdown ever, but it was not called a "touchdown" then. Although all the parts of the story cannot be proven, it is known that after his unusual play, the sport of football began to change. Players decided that the game could be improved.

They agreed on some new rules to make the game more fun and challenging. A player should be allowed to carry or run with the ball. Also, to be fair, his opponents must be permitted to stop him. That meant they could tackle and pull a runner to the ground. Since a player carrying the ball could not outrun everyone on the other team, his teammates would be allowed to protect him. That meant teammates could block opposing players trying to tackle their runner. The new plays of tackling and blocking were added to the game, and they changed the sport significantly.

The game that had been played in England for hundreds of years eventually became three separate games. The old game where players mainly kicked the ball became the sport that is known in America today as soccer, although it is still called football outside of Canada

An illustration depicts students at the Rugby School in England in 1845 playing a version of the game that became modern football.

and the United States. The new game in which the ball could be carried was named rugby after William's school. In North America, people started playing a third game, one that combined parts of the other two. It came to be called American football.

A Rough and Tough Game

Today the game of American football is big, loud, and rowdy. Some people think that is exactly why the country loves it. They say Americans admire strong competition and winning after a hard fight, and football delivers all that and more. Some fans love the fast action combined with the crisp fall weather, the socializing, and eating football-party fare with family and friends. Others admire the athletes because of their speed, strength, and endurance. There are also fans who admit they cannot describe how they feel about football, but they cannot imagine life without it. Joe Namath, the professional quarterback elected to the Football Hall of Fame in 1985, summed up his love for the game. "Football is an honest game. It's true to life. It's a game about sharing. Football is a team game. So is life."[1]

For many reasons, America is obsessed with football. It is the country's most popular spectator sport. More people play basketball, baseball, and soccer on local teams, but when it comes to what game to watch, football is the clear winner. Mary McGrory (1918–2004), a columnist for *The Washington Star* and *The Washington Post,* wrote, "Baseball is what we were, football is what we have become."[2]

The Super Bowl, the championship game of the 32-team National Football League (NFL), is the largest yearly sporting event in the country. Television poll takers estimate that half the nation watches it. In cities all over the country, millions of people also watch college football and attend local high school games.

In many towns and rural areas, citizens show fanatic loyalty to their local

EXTRA POINT

1952

The first year Willie Thrower, the first African American quarterback in the NFL, played for the Chicago Bears.

Super Bowl Parties

20 million Americans join friends at Super Bowl parties.

17 is the average number of people at each party.

11 million pounds of potato chips are consumed on Super Bowl Sunday.

13 million pounds of avocados are used to make guacamole.

3 million pounds of popcorn are popped.

high school teams and make games important social events. From the open tailgates of their vehicles, they host parties and serve picnic food. The games feature cheerleading squads that lead spirit-raising chants and marching bands that play uplifting tunes at halftime. People visit with one another and root together for their team. Fans discuss plays and players, get mad at the referees, and scream with joy or shake their heads in disgust when the game ends.

American's love of football seems to go beyond just the games they attend or watch. Vince Lombardi, the famous coach of the Green Bay Packers, felt the same way. He said, "The spirit, the will to win and the will to excel … these are the qualities that are so much more important than any of the events themselves."[3] Because football is more than just a game to Americans, its influence has spread into other areas of American culture.

Off the Field

Football has been featured in the movies since the early days of film, even before movies had sound. In 1925 The Harold Lloyd Corporation released *The Freshman*, a silent comedy. The film tells the story of a college freshman trying to become popular by joining the school football team and making a fool of himself. More than sixty movies about football have been made. Two films chosen by fans as among the best are

Friday Night Lights, a 2004 film starring Billy Bob Thornton as a high school football coach in Texas, is one of many popular movies made about the sport.

Friday Night Lights (2004, Universal Pictures) and *Brian's Song* (1971, Sony Pictures Home Entertainment). In *Friday Night Lights,* players live in a town where succeeding at football is the only way out of poverty. The pressure to win is intense. While working hard, team members learn that there is more to winning than the final score of the game. *Brian's Song* was inspired by real life and tells the story of a player's fight with cancer and a friendship that outshines football, race, and hard times.

In addition to influencing movies, football has had an affect on everyday language. The phrase "drop back" means to move back behind the offensive line in order to pass or run around the end. People use it also to describe someone who's avoiding people. "She was embarrassed and dropped back behind the group." "Huddle" is what the offensive team does when it gathers closely together to decide on the next play. It is also used when people consult about other things. "Let's huddle and decide what to do." "Touchdown" is used to mean winning or achieving in anything. "Kick-off" is used for the starting time of parties, work projects, and meals or to mean the beginning of something new.

America's love of the game has "kicked-off" a new kind of football game. Fantasy Football has gained tremendous popularity in America. It is played by more than 30 million Americans, and the numbers keep growing. A group of about ten fans gets together and draft real NFL players as members of their make-believe team. The fantasy teams compete with each other weekly. What a real player does in a real game determines the points he earns for the fantasy teams he is on. The points are based on such things as how many touch-downs, interceptions, or how much yardage is earned.

Football in all its forms is an important part of American society. It appeals to the country's spirit of teamwork, competition, and striving to achieve. Yet the game that is so much a part of life today has changed a lot since it was brought from England and first played at schools in the United States.

American Football Grows Up

In the mid-1800s, American football was played mostly in the colleges and universities. Because traveling then was hard and expensive, schools did not play each other. Teams made up their own rules that were followed on their campus, but rules varied a lot between schools. Some schools allowed the game to be quite violent, while other schools had strict rules against rough playing and even punished students for using too much force.

The universities of Princeton and Rutgers were located a few miles from each other in New Jersey. They were big rivals and played pranks back and forth trying to better each other. On November 6, 1869, their football teams went against each other in the first football game between two U.S. colleges. The game differed greatly from a modern football game. The ball was round not oblong, and twenty-five men played on each side of the field. Teams could only make one point at a time by kicking the ball between the two posts at each end of the field. A player could not run with the ball. He kicked or dribbled with his feet, or he batted it with his feet, hands, head, and sides of his body. A line of blockers protected the man as he advanced the ball. Although Princeton had the most muscle, Rutgers players kicked better and won the match.

As football became popular, more universities in the United States and Canada played. When Harvard University went up against McGill University from Canada for two games, they played the first game by McGill rules and the second one by Harvard rules. Afterwards, the Harvard players decided they liked the boisterous McGill game better. They also like the egg-shaped ball they used. Under McGill rules, they could run with the football and cross the finish line to touch it on the ground. The McGill players called this

A statue on the campus of Rutgers University commemorates the first college football game played between Rutgers and rival Princeton University on November 6, 1869.

a "touchdown." Harvard players adopted this new word and most of McGill's rules.

The Father of American Football

At Yale university, coach Walter Camp put more modern ideas into practice. In 1880, he invented the scrimmage line and the rule that only one team at a time could have possession of the ball. In rugby, players struggled over the ball in a kind of free-for-all. Under Camp's rules, one player put the ball into play by snapping it (quickly passing it backwards between his legs) to another player who served as the quarterback. One team had possession of the ball for a set number of downs and distance. These new rules made it necessary to mark off a field every five yards. This marking the field off in a grid pattern led to American football being called the "gridiron" game. Gridiron football is played today with eleven men to a side, four downs, and a 100-yard field.

Amos Stagg

Amos Stagg (1862–1965) gained fame as a player at Yale and then went on to coach football at the University of Chicago. Walter Camp was responsible for the changes that made American football unique, but Amos Stagg did more to popularize the game. He came up with clever new ideas, like the tackling dummy, a large foam shape that can be used for tackling practice.

He invented the tricky Statue of Liberty play. In this play, the quarterback draws his arms back as if to throw the ball. While one arm carries through with the fake throwing motion, the other arm slides the ball behind his back and hands it off to a running back or receiver going by. Stagg also thought up the famous turtleback formation, which became standard for the game. For this strategy, a team drove toward the defense in an oval formation. Later the formation became a T shape. The center and quarterback made up the trunk of the T, while the backs formed the top of the T.

THE FOOTBALL FIELD

In American football two teams of 11 line up facing each other. The team trying to score is called offense. The team trying to prevent scoring is called defense. This diagram shows a typical formation in which offensive and defensive players line up along the line of scrimmage.

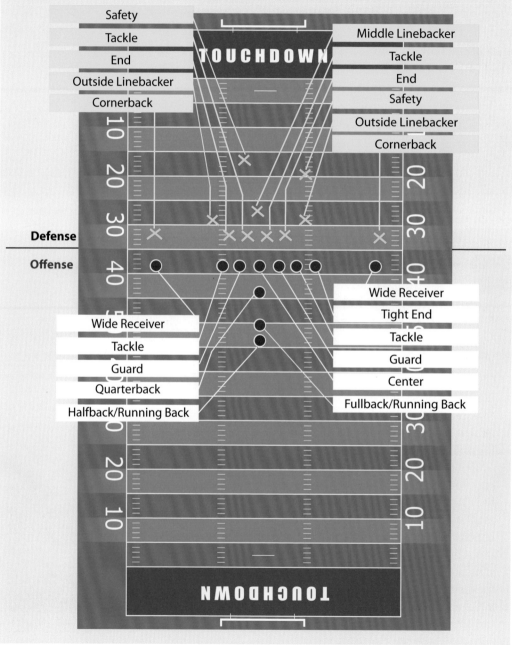

The scoring system back then gave more points to kicking a ball over the goal posts (field goal) than to running or throwing the ball over the goal line (touchdown). By the early 1890s, touchdowns and field goals earned equal points. Two other big changes had also been made. Traditionally tackling had been allowed only from the waist up, which was the practice in rugby. Players now started tackling each other as low as the knees. Plus, linemen and blockers were no longer allowed to hold their arms out and link them to form a ring of men to protect the runner.

Soon there was a new rule about throwing a pass. Earlier rugby rules required that a player had to throw a ball so it traveled backwards. Passing a ball did not gain ground for a team. By 1905 the forward pass received official approval.

As universities scheduled regular matches against each other, more and more players got hurt. Harvard's flying wedge play caused many injuries. For the wedge play, suitcase handles were sewn onto the backs of linemen's shirts. With the ball carrier sheltered behind them, the linemen grabbed each other's back handles and pounded down the field as a solid wedge of men.

Dangerous plays caused hundreds of serious injuries, and several men died. Many colleges banned the sport at their schools, and President Theodore Roosevelt threatened to ban it nationwide. He had played college football and loved it, but the game had become far too dangerous. Together universities outlawed the most hazardous plays, and the games continued.

Though sometimes risky, the sport had grown in popularity. Athletic clubs had started competing against one anther locally, and a few football stars had become professional players.

Pro Football

When several Pittsburgh clubs took up football, they took winning very seriously. The Alleghany Athletic Association paid William Heffelfinger $500 to play on their team. He was a football celebrity from Yale, who went by the

EXTRA POINT

1986
The first season instant replays were used to decide if the original call was correct

nickname of Pudge. He helped the Alleghany team beat the Pittsburgh Athletic Association in 1892. That made Heffelfinger the first man to be paid for playing on a team—the first football professional football player. Charles Follis, called the Black Cyclone, signed a contract in 1902 with the Shelby Athletic Club in Shelby, Ohio. He became the sport's first black professional.

In 1899 Chris O'Brien started a team that is still around today. He named his team the Chicago Cardinals, but it later came to be called the St. Louis Cardinals and then the Arizona Cardinals of the National Football League. The Cardinals team is the oldest professional team still playing today. The first owner of a football team was William Temple, who put all his players on the payroll in 1900.

The National Football League

In 1920 the American Professional Football Association (APFA) was formed in Canton, Ohio. The next year its name changed to the National Football League. The Providence Steam Rollers and the Framingham Lion Tamers were two teams in the association. The Oolong Indians, whose members were all Native Americans, also belonged to the league.

Fans of the Detroit Lions cheer on their team. They are among millions of Americans who turn out to support their favorite professional, college, or high-school teams each week during football season.

The Vince Lombardi Trophy

The Super Bowl trophy, also called the Vince Lombardi trophy, starts as a mound of sterling silver. Since 1966, the jewelry making company Tiffany & Co. has crafted the trophy at a special silversmith shop in Parsippany, N.J. Bill Testra is employed there as a master spinner. He works over a flat disc revolving at high speed. Using a 1,200-degree blowtorch, he creates the shape of the football from two sterling silver plates. Then another Tiffany employee, Joe Laczko, solders the halves together. The trophy is twenty-two inches (56cm) tall and weighs seven pounds (3.2kg). The words "Vince Lombardi Trophy" are engraved on it. It is awarded on the field after each Super Bowl, then it goes back to Tiffany's so it can be engraved with the name of the winning team, the date, and the final score.

Green Bay Packers quarterback Aaron Rodgers holds the Vince Lombardi Trophy after winning Super Bowl XLV in 2011.

Today thirty-two teams make up the NFL, which is divided into two conferences, the American Football Conference (AFC) and the National Football Conference (NFC). Each conference has sixteen teams, four in each division: east, west, north, and south. The NFL season goes for seventeen weeks between September and December or January. During that time, each team plays a total of sixteen games. At the end of the season, twelve teams (six from each conference) have earned the right to compete in the NFL playoffs. If a team loses a game, it is eliminated from playing anymore for the championship. Two teams (one from each conference) go on to play in the Super Bowl, which is the NFL championship.

A professional football game anywhere in the country will usually attract more than 60,000 fans. Of all the professional sports leagues in the United States, the NFL has the highest attendance for events. Although football is mainly a male sport, it is estimated that about one-fourth of the fans are female. Women and girls also play the game, and their numbers are growing. Only a few high schools or colleges offer football just for girls or women, but females are sometimes allowed to play on the male team. Several leagues dedicated to female players have formed since 2000.

Women, Girls, and Gridiron

The Women's American Flag Football Federation promotes flag football for women and girls throughout the United States and Canada. Flag football is popular all over the world and not just played by women. Instead of tackling players to end a down, the defensive team must remove a flag or flag belt from the ball carrier.

Women also take part in full-contact football. The women's leagues go by the same rules that men do, but females use a slightly smaller ball. Most teams are semi-professional or amateur. The Women's Football Alliance (WFA), based in Visalia, California, is the fastest growing women's football tour worldwide. It boasts more than 100 teams in the United States and all over the world.

Football is a pleasure, a pastime, and a passion for millions of Americans, and fans across the globe are just as obsessed with all varieties of the game.

Football Around the World

Rugby, soccer, and American football are played in countless countries. Rugby has two variations, rugby league and rugby union, and both are played professionally in the United States and many other nations. For the first time ever, rugby union teams will compete in the 2016 Olympic Games in Rio de Janeiro.

Association football, called soccer in the United States and Canada, is the world's most popular sport. The game is played today according to rules that were published in 1863. Its championship game, the World Cup, is held every four years.

People in fifty-two countries on five continents play American football. The International Federation of American Football (IFAF), formed in 1998, declared Japan its first world champion when it defeated Mexico in 1999.

All forms of football require strength, speed, and stamina. They also require strategy and quick thinking. Knute Rockne, the legendary coach of Notre Dame's football team, agreed that football takes brainpower. He said, "Football is a game played with arms, legs and shoulders but mostly from the neck up."[4] Yet there is a false belief that has refused to go away in America. It is the idea that football players are big, brawny, and stupid.

The Myth of the Dumb Jock

In 2004 the National Collegiate Athletic Association (NCAA) did a study that compared students who were not athletes to students who were. Their results disprove the notion that athletes are not as intelligent as other students. Student athletes graduated at higher rates and earned more advanced college degrees. More of them were employed than those who had not played sports, and they earned higher salaries.

Joe Montana, who was elected to the Pro Football Hall of Fame in 2000, wrote in his autobiography that all teams have huge, strong players, but he said brains are often the difference between winning and losing. "Stop thinking, start losing,"[5] he wrote.

Grit for the Gridiron: Training

Although playing a competitive game of football takes strategy, a conditioned body is an absolute necessity. Football is a tough game. Players need rigorous training if they hope to perform well and avoid injury. Sportscaster Frank Gifford, a former NFL player, described the game this way. "Pro football is like nuclear warfare. There are no winners, only survivors."[6] A good football training program includes strength, speed, endurance, and agility conditioning for all players, as well as training for the specific positions played.

The various positions in football require different skills and types of strength. Quarterbacks need to build arm strength. They must also be able to move quickly so that after the ball is snapped from the center to the quarterback, they can scramble free of opposition to throw a pass. Both offensive and defensive linemen have to be big and powerful to hold strong against the opposition, so they work on bulk and overall strength. Wide receivers build up their legs so they can jump and catch a pass. They also work on quickness and speed drills. They must move fast to avoid the defensive backs whose job it is to prevent them from catching passes and running toward the end zone. Former NFL head coach John Madden said, "There is a difference in being in shape and being in football shape. Anyone can go out on the field and run around, but once you start getting hit and have to get up then you find out the difference between being in shape and football shape."[7] No matter what position is being played, football conditioning starts with strength training, which focuses on the skeletal muscles.

Skeletal Muscles

The human body has three types of muscles. There is the cardiac muscle of the heart, the smooth muscles of organs like the stomach and lungs, and the skeletal muscles. Skeletal muscles provide power and strength for the body to move. There are more than 630 of them in the human body, and they come in various sizes and shapes that serve specific purposes. Some of the major skeletal muscles are the large, powerful ones near the spine. They make it possible for a person to stand upright, while they also supply the power

The human muscular system. Players need to build major body movers like the shoulders, back, and leg muscles along with stabilizing muscles like the abdomen and arms.

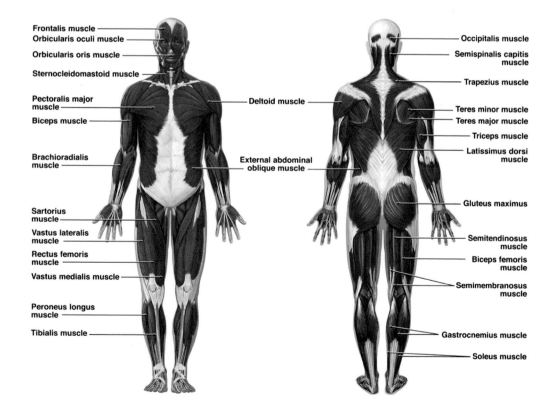

Frontalis muscle
Orbicularis oculi muscle
Orbicularis oris muscle
Sternocleidomastoid muscle
Pectoralis major muscle
Biceps muscle
Brachioradialis muscle
Sartorius muscle
Vastus lateralis muscle
Rectus femoris muscle
Vastus medialis muscle
Peroneus longus muscle
Tibialis muscle

Deltoid muscle
External abdominal oblique muscle

Occipitalis muscle
Semispinalis capitis muscle
Trapezius muscle
Teres minor muscle
Teres major muscle
Triceps muscle
Latissimus dorsi muscle
Gluteus maximus
Semitendinosus muscle
Biceps femoris muscle
Semimembranosus muscle
Gastrocnemius muscle
Soleus muscle

to push against an opposing player in a football game. Other major skeletal muscles are the deltoid muscles that move the shoulders; and the biceps that flex the arms. The deltoids and biceps enable a quarterback to throw a football. Each side of the upper chest has a pectoral muscle, which are often called "pecs." A muscular chest adds to the overall body strength and bulk of a player. They help a lineman block. The rectus abdominus muscles are in front of the abdomen and stomach and are referred to as "abs." A strong abdomen improves balance and guards against lower back injuries. The quadriceps or "quads" are the large muscles on the front of the thighs, and the hamstrings are on the back of the thighs. These muscles help a player run, jump, and kick and aid in maintaining good balance while on the field. The gluteus maximus is the muscle on the buttocks. Strong glutes help with running, jumping, and changing position.

All skeletal muscles are voluntary muscles, which are the ones a person intentionally controls. Voluntary muscles only respond when a player decides to pass the ball, run down the field, or block an opponent and the brain sends a message to the muscles to act. A player can make skeletal muscles stronger and bigger through exercise, and this happens because of the way the body heals injured muscle tissue.

Building Muscle

Threadlike fibers make up muscle tissue. When muscle bulks up, it is because each individual fiber in the muscle grew in size. When a football player exercises a certain muscle group, the purpose is to overwork the muscles just a little and cause mild damage to the fibers. As the body quickly heals the fibers, it makes the newly repaired tissue stronger than before. It also makes the new tissue a little bit bigger. As an athlete continues to exercise, this process happens over and over, and a player's muscles become larger and stronger.

According to Troy Hatton, the football strength and conditioning coordinator at the University of New Mexico, bulk and strength are important for linemen. He says, "Offensive and defensive lineman require the most weight. They are the largest players on the team. These are our front men. They

are in the trenches protecting the quarterback or trying to get to the opposing team's quarterback."[8]

Bodybuilding exercises cause a gain in lean weight and bulk, but they are not the best method for increasing overall strength. A bodybuilder's goal is to build up his visible muscles, making them look larger and more defined. Football players are concerned with training both the muscles that can be seen and those that cannot. They aim for overall body strength, not necessarily size or definition. They focus on working the prime muscles and keeping them in balance to work together with equal effort. If one muscle or group of muscles works harder than it should while others fail to work hard enough, muscular imbalance occurs. This causes soreness, decreased energy, and sometimes injuries. Football players need to build major body movers like shoulder, back, and leg muscles equally with stabilizing muscles like the abdomen, chest, and arms. Players build overall strength and balance with resistance exercises.

Oakland Raiders wide receiver Jerry Porter flexes his bicep muscle before a game in 2007. Football players engage in workouts designed to build muscle in order to increase strength and improve balance.

Mind Over Muscle

Experiments done at the Cleveland Clinic Foundation showed that a muscle is strengthened after a person has just thought about exercising it. Thirty young adults took part in the study that lasted for twelve weeks. All they did was think about moving their little fingers or their elbows. They did this for five minutes a day five days a week. They were told to think as hard as they could about moving the muscle and to imagine the movement as if it really happened. A control group that did no imaginary exercises showed no increase in strength. However, the group that imagined moving their little fingers showed a thirty-five percent gain in finger strength. Those who imagined moving their elbows had an increase of thirteen percent in strength. Also, brain scans taken after the study revealed that the brain had improved in its ability to signal muscle.

Resistance Exercises

While doing resistance exercises, a person performs an effort against an opposing force, and the opposing force makes the muscles contract. When an athlete does push-ups, his own body weight supplies the resistance. The goal is to strengthen skeletal muscles. Many of the exercises are designed to use multiple joints and muscles in a coordinated, smooth movement. This type of exercise develops a football player's ability to push and pull and to supply resistance against getting pushed or pulled by an opposing player.

For some resistance exercises, an athlete uses moderate weights and frequent repetitions that focus on one muscle group. Then the player switches to an exercise that targets another muscle group. Dumbbells, weight machines, and elastic bands are often used. A common exercise is the power clean. In this exercise, the athlete bends his knees, grips a barbell on the floor, and steadily lifts it to his waist and then to his shoulders. To do this properly, there should no jerking, the barbell should always be under control, and the feet are in line when the barbell is raised to the shoulders.

STRENGTH TRAINING EXERCISES

Four basic exercises that football players use to build overall strength are the power clean, squats, lunges, and bench press.

Power clean

Bench press

Squat

Lunge

Aaron Wellman is the football strength and conditioning coach at San Diego State University in California. He has athletes build upper body muscles by using hand weights and doing bench press exercises on a power rack. The power rack is a piece of equipment that allows someone to safely lift heavy barbells. An athlete lies on a bench that has a barbell supported on bars above his head. He unracks or lifts the barbell off the support bars, lowers it to his chest, presses it back up until his arms are straight, and returns it to rest again on the support bars. Wellman's players build lower body strength by doing leg squat exercises. These involve bending the knees and lowering the body while holding a barbell across the shoulders. Players also do leg lunges. The player lowers the body by stepping out on one leg and bending both knees. Lunges can also be done while holding weights. These drills are rotated with other exercises, like running track.

Trainers also set up specific exercises for players based on the positions they play, and these can include resistance exercises. A common exercise for building leg strength is doing leg curls on a leg machine, something wide receivers spend extra time doing. To develop better kicking skills, Troy Hatton has his players use the four way hip machine and hurdles, focusing on the hip and groin areas. For quarterbacks, he says, "We concentrate on strengthening the throwing muscles, the rotator cuff and the shoulder girth."[9]

In 2009 Cincinnati Bengals quarterback Carson Palmer explained how he planned to improve his arm strength. "To get your arm in shape you throw and continue to throw. So I will be throwing all summer long as well as in training camp."[10] A drill some quarterbacks use is the long ball drill. From about ten yards away, the quarterback throws the ball to a receiver. Accuracy is important, and with each throw of this drill he aims to hit the receiver at the same place—for example, just under the chin. After three throws, the quarterback backs up another ten yards. He continues this routine until his throws no longer reach the receiver.

Ancient Gyms

The ancient Greeks took pride in staying in excellent physical shape. They ran and threw the discus and javelin, but they also had gymnasiums to exercise in. There were rooms for wrestling, a common form of competitive exercise. There was only one rule—no eye gouging. Everything else was allowed. In the exercise rooms, men could whack a "korykos," which was like the modern punching bag.

It was a large leather sack filled with sand, flour, or fig-grains. Athletes played various kinds of ball and a tug of war game with a rope to build strength. The gyms also had areas for talking and bathing.

A marble relief from ancient Greece depicts two athletes wrestling. Physical fitness and competitive sports were highly valued in ancient Greek society.

Then he throws the ball three more times as far as he can and stops. The goal is to practice without making the arm sore or numb. In another drill, the player throws a weighted ball using great force.

Along with practicing specific skills and building strength, increasing speed and endurance are important for players.

Speed and Endurance

Troy Hatton says speed and power are most important for skill position players, those who catch the football and those who run with it—the quarterback, running back, tight end, wide receiver, linebacker, and defensive back. "Our three main goals are strength, power and speed," he says about the training program. "We also want to optimize each player's body type."[11] Speed is crucial for running backs, wide receivers, and defensive backs. Once off the line, a defensive lineman needs to keep moving rapidly to get to the quarterback. A football player wants to increase his running speed and his

A ball carrier relies on speed in order to achieve top performance. Muscle contraction, not strength, is a factor in speed, so football players look to build up their fast-twitch muscle fibers.

endurance, which is how long muscles can perform and keep up an activity. He also aims to increase his rate of acceleration, which is how quickly he can reach his maximum speed. Some trainers have players focus on exercises that work the two kinds of muscle fibers in different ways.

Muscle fibers are divided into fibers that contract slowly and fibers that contract quickly. The quicker fibers are called fast-twitch fibers. They are thicker and more powerful, and they contract two to three times faster than slow-twitch muscles. Trainers say sprinting speed is based on how fast muscles contract, not how strong they are. When football players build up more fast-twitch muscle fibers, they are better at plays that need short spurts of action. They are faster and reach their maximum speed more quickly. Athletes train fast-twitch fibers by increasing the load of the weights they lift during a workout. They begin with a lighter weight and do many repetitions, then they add more weight for the next sets and do fewer repetitions. This kind of workout is intense, and players must allow one to two days recovery time before another session.

Even though fast-twitch fibers give muscles speed and quick bursts of strength, they also tire faster, and a football player must have muscular endurance to last during sixty minutes of activity. A defensive back must be prepared to travel ten to fifteen yards during every play. By the fourth quarter when the fast-twitch fibers have tired, the slower ones give the athlete the staying power he needs. Even though the slow-twitch fibers do not get as large, they do not tire as quickly as fast-twitch fibers. They are used for actions that require endurance, but do not need as much power. To train slow-twitch fibers, players lift weights that are under the maximum weight they can hold, but they slowly increase the number of repetitions. Trainers want players to condition both their fast-twitch fibers and slow-twitch fibers since speed and endurance are equally important. Players also work to improve agility and flexibility, which are a crucial part of physical fitness for football players.

Agility and Flexibility

"From the largest to the smallest player, we are looking for agility," says Troy Hatton. "Agility combines all of the characteristics that are important in an effective athlete—balance, coordination, reaction, speed, etc. We spend a great deal of time on running mechanics, footwork, and speed drills to improve quickness and agility."[12]

Agility is being able to change direction quickly, whether it is reversing the whole body or the direction of the arms or legs. Offensive and defensive linemen must get off the line fast, and quarterbacks and runners also need to be fast, agile, and flexible. After the ball is snapped, a quarterback must scramble free of opposition to throw a pass. Agility training for all players is one of the most important elements of a conditioning program and includes exercises to make an athlete more flexible or limber.

For a common agility exercise, two cones are put on a field a few yards away from each other. Then one by one, players run around and between the cones in a figure eight pattern. Another routine trains players to be ready for the snap of the ball. For this exercise, the coach holds the

Members of the Washington Redskins' defensive line stretch their muscles before a workout session. Proper stretching improves a player's flexibility and agility.

football and stands between two players. Then he acts as if he is snapping the ball as the center would to the quarterback. Immediately the two players race and try to beat each other to a marker five or ten yards away. Jumping, skipping, jumping rope, hopping, lunges, and jump squats are also common drills that strengthen muscles and improve agility and flexibility.

Flexibility is the ability of muscle tissue to extend or stretch and reach its greatest range of motion. An inflexible body makes it hard for a football player to race for a touchdown, kick the ball correctly, and jump as high as needed to grab a catch out of the air. Muscles stretch and contract like a rubber band. The more they are stretched, the more elastic and workable they become. A muscle can become so overdeveloped and bulky that it stays flexed or extended and cannot contract. This is called being "muscle bound," and a muscle in this condition is actually weak even if it is large and looks strong. Many bodybuilders are muscle bound. A muscle bound football player would have limited range of motion and could not punt well. He would not be able to react quickly on the field and turn rapidly. Also when a player is tackled, the more flexible his body is the less likely he is to be injured. Football players do exercises to stretch all parts of their bodies to improve agility and flexibility. An agile, flexible football player can block better, sprint faster, and kick with expert precision and do it with less harm to his body.

Stronger and Safer

Aaron Wellman trains players so they can become stronger and faster, but his main goal of conditioning is to prevent injuries. He says there are three main things that contribute to a player getting hurt.

1. A high level of body fat. Too much body fat causes a player to get fatigued faster, and a tired player is more likely to get hurt.
2. Training too hard for too long. "Football training has changed over the past twenty years," Wellman says. "Players took a lot more time off. Now they train all year with just a little time off."[13] But he also says that players should not overdo training. They must have enough time for their bodies to recover between exercise sessions.
3. Muscular imbalance on the body. If a player's quads are bigger than his hamstrings, he has an imbalance in his legs. A muscular imbalance causes the body to be less flexible and stable which can lead to injury on the field.

Dave Binder serves as the Head Athletics Trainer at the University of New Mexico. He says, "We warm up extensively before each game and we work hard on conditioning so that our athletes are prepared for the game. We hope that when the game starts, our athletes are ready to go and prepared to work the entire game."[14]

Athletes practice and train almost every day. Bill Parcells coached the Dallas Cowboys and led the New York Giants to two Super Bowl wins. Before the first game of the year, he reminded his players, "Hey fellas! This is what you work all off season for. This is why you lift all them weights! This is why you do all that!"[15]

CHAPTER 3

The Perfect Arc: Passing, Punting, and Kicking

When an NFL player passes the ball in a game, he uses his skill and experience to throw like a pro. He instinctively considers several things before he throws the ball. If the receiver is standing close, he does not throw the ball as hard or as high. If the receiver is some distance away, the thrower puts more energy into the toss and throws the ball higher or at a more vertical angle. The thrower is applying natural laws without pondering them. If he did think about them, mechanics would be on his mind. Mechanics is the branch of physics that studies motion. Whether it is being thrown, punted, or fumbled, the shape of the ball, along with the laws of motion and gravity, affect how it moves.

An Aerodynamic Ball

According to the rules of professional and college football, the outside of a football must be made of leather. Four strips of leather are sewn together with strong laces to cover a rubber bladder, which is inflated to 12.5 to 13.5 pounds per square inch (psi; .87to.94kPa). The modern football has a stretched-out roundish shape with points at the end. The mathematical name of the shape is a prolate spheroid. The pointed ends give it an aerodynamic shape, or one that moves easily through the air. The reason the shape helps it to fly smoothly has to do with a factor called wake. When a ball soars, it leaves a wake or patch of stirred-up air behind where it cut through. The tapered ends of the football means that a narrow wake is made. Less air is stirred up so there is less air drag on the ball. Air drag is the friction or resistance caused by air going over an object as the object moves through it and the ball collides with molecules in the air. The drag force is related to the amount of area that the ball puts forward to the air speeding by. A perfectly round ball like a soccer ball leaves behind a wider wake and experiences greater air drag.

The oblong shape of a football makes the ball spiral when kicked or thrown correctly. A spiraling football encounters less air drag than a ball thrown without spin. This is because a ball that is not spinning will wobble. A wobbling ball puts forward more surface area toward the air as it travels, which means there is more drag on the ball. A spiraling football twists through the air in a tight coil or corkscrew manner. A tight spiraling pattern means that a smaller surface area of the ball hits the wind head-on as the ball cuts through the air.

How a football bounces is less predictable than how it flies. Bud Grant, head coach to the Minnesota Vikings (NFL) for eighteen years, said, "There are coaches who

Regulation Pigskins

The NCAA and the NFL have the same specifications for footballs.

Short Circumference: 20.75 to 21.25 inches (52.7 to 54cm)
Long Circumference: 28 to 28.5 inches (71.1 to 72.4cm)
Weight: approximately 14 to 15 oz (397 to 425g)

spend eighteen hours a day coaching the perfect game and they lose because the ball is oval and they can't control the bounce." [16] If a kicked ball lands on its side, it will bounce like a soccer ball. Yet if it lands on one of the pointed ends, a player scrambling to catch it may find it bouncing away out of his grasp. When a player lets the ball slip from his hands, it can also bounce in multiple ways.

Although a bouncing football may go where a player wishes it would not, all mass in motion follows certain laws of physics that were studied and defined more than three hundred years ago.

Mass in Motion

Sir Isaac Newton (1643–1727) developed theories about the physics of motion, light, and gravity. The famous scientist and mathematician is considered the father of modern physics. Among his many contributions to science are his three laws of motion. His first law states: An object at rest tends to stay at rest, and an object in motion tends to stay in motion at the same speed and in the same direction, unless acted upon by an unbalanced force. This means that mass does not change what it is doing and continues on with the same action, unless another force acts upon it. A football at rest on a grassy yard will stay just as it is unless force is applied to one side but not the other (unbalanced force). If someone stands so the football is between his shoes and applies equal pressure to both sides of the ball (providing balanced force), it will not move. But if someone kicks the football, it will move because unbalanced force has been applied to one side. If the football rolls into the street, it will keep rolling until some force like gravity or friction stops it. The football would only stop rolling because gravity or friction put an unbalanced force against it.

Newton's second law states: The greater the mass of an object, the greater the force needed to move the object. Force is the thing that speeds an object up or slows it down and can be measured by the equation: Force equals mass times acceleration (F = ma). Mass is related to the weight of an object. Acceleration is the change in the speed an object is traveling. It is figured by first calculating the velocity, which

Two football players colliding with each other each exert the same amount of force, according to Newton's Third Law.

Sir Isaac Newton

Sir Isaac Newton (1643–1727) was an English mathematician, physicist, astronomer, philosopher, and alchemist, a kind of medieval chemist that tried to convert common metals into precious metals. His father died before he was born, and he worked on his mother's farm as a young man before attending Trinity College in Cambridge. He created a type of calculus and changed views about geometry. His theories about light and sound and his explanations of gravity brought him worldwide fame. Newton served as president of the Royal Society and Master of the Mint, where he worked to expose and prevent counterfeiting. He even gathered evidence for cases by wearing a disguise and hanging out in taverns. Queen Anne honored him with a knighthood in 1705. Newton is considered to be one of the greatest scientists and mathematicians who ever lived.

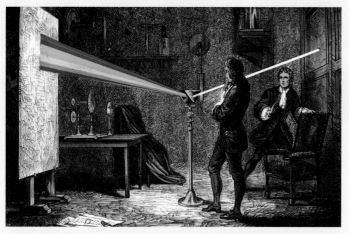

English scientist and mathematician Sir Isaac Newton conducts an experiment using light and a prism.

is the speed and direction an object travels. To get velocity, the distance the object travels is divided by the amount of time it takes to get there. There is an equation to figure acceleration based on the starting velocity, final velocity, and the time it takes to reach the final velocity.

Newton's second law can be understood by comparing the force needed to kick a football with the force needed to kick a ping pong ball. Greater force is required to move a football which is about 15 ounces (425g) than to move a ping pong ball which is only .09 ounces (2.7g).

Newton's third law states: For every action, there is an equal and opposite reaction. This means that when two masses collide or two football players smash together, they exert the same amount of force on one another but they do it in opposite directions. This may not seem logical. It seems that a bigger player would put more force on a smaller player. Yet when force is concerned in an impact, it does not matter if one body weighs more or is going faster. The two bodies receive equal force in opposite directions. One player may go flying afterwards, and one may not, but that is due to other factors that involve things like the length of time of the impact. It is not due to unequal force. When two colliding bodies have different masses, the equal forces will cause different accelerations.

Kicking the Ball

When a football is thrown or kicked at an angle and travels through the air, it always follows a curved path that has specific mathematical properties. The Italian physicist, Galileo (1564–1642), discovered this concept of projectile motion. A projectile is an object, like a football, a cannonball, or an arrow, launched into the air by a force. Galileo reasoned that an object in flight is affected by two different motions, horizontal motion and vertical motion. The force of gravity pulls down on the object vertically while the object continues to travel forward or horizontally. As the object goes up, gravity slows it down until it stops very briefly at its highest point. Then the object comes down, and the pull of gravity makes it accelerate until it hits the ground. Galileo was able to show that gravity and the thrust forward work together to create a U-shaped curve. The curve, called a parabola, has specific mathematical properties. The exact path of the object can be determined using a mathematical formula that takes into account the speed and angle of the object when it was released.

PHYSICS OF A KICK

When he kicks the ball, a player controls three things: the velocity at which the ball leaves his foot, the angle of the kick, and the rotation of the football. Kicking also uses the principle of conservation of momentum. The initial momentum of the kicker's leg and the ball before the kicker's foot meets the ball equals the final momentum and energy after the collision. That momentum and energy are transferred to the ball, which launches it into the air.

The kicker increases his velocity as he approaches the ball.

When he is near the ball, he plants his non-kicking foot firmly on the ground.

With the non-kicking foot firmly planted next to the ball, the kicker swings his kicking leg in a wide arc and then straightens the leg as his foot makes contact with the ball.

The player's mass and acceleration create the force that propels the ball into the air.

Hanging in the Wind

When he kicks, a punter controls three things: the velocity at which the ball leaves his foot, the angle of the kick, and the rotation of the football. He lets the ball drop toward the ground and before it can land, he kicks—making contact with the ball using the part of his foot between the toe and ankle. The velocity and angle of the kick determine how high and how far the ball will go. They also determine hang time, or the amount of time the ball spends in the air. A punter wants to the ball to stay in the air as long as possible because a long hang time gives his teammates a better chance of getting down the field in time to tackle the receiver.

The punter also tries to make the ball fly in a tight spiral or spin. A ball that is spiraling will stay in the air longer and go farther than an end-over-end kick. If he kicks with the right leg, the player creates the spiral motion by kicking from right to left across the lower part of the ball. Good punters succeed in producing some kind of spiraling flight in the ball about 80 percent of the time. When a ball flies in a tight

Cleveland Browns placekicker Phil Dawson strides towards the ball during a field goal attempt in 2011. The accuracy of a kick is dependent upon several factors, including wind conditions, the angle to the goal, and the steadiness of the hold.

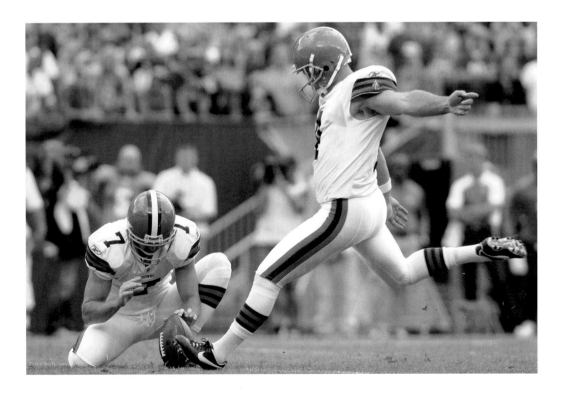

spin, it rotates around its long axis, the invisible line that goes from tip to tip. As the ball flies, the long axis will stay pointing along the line of the ball's path. If the ball spirals but also wobbles, its long axis or tip may not point along the path of the ball, but may point more upward, and the ball may land on its side instead of on one point.

One problem kickers have is that making the ball cover a long distance on the field works against hang time. With all balls, not just a football, launching it at a 45-degree angle causes the ball to fly the farthest range, yet kicking it at a 50-degree angle means the ball will hang in the air longer. According to the laws of projectile motion, the higher the angle of the kick, the longer it will take for the ball to come down. Launching the ball straight up at a 90-degree angle allows for the longest possible hang time, but that does not move the football down the field.

When a player prepares to kick the ball, he must consider where he is on the field in order to decide on the best angle to launch. Punters and placekickers also pay attention to wind conditions. A strong breeze can make the ball veer or alter course in midair. It is harder for a placekicker to execute just the right angle for a field goal because the ball often reaches its top height and starts down before it reaches the goal posts. Field goal kickers are even more concerned about the effects of wind because they must land the ball in a specific place—between the uprights.

When a player placekicks a ball to start the game or for a field goal, another player holds the ball in place or the ball is placed on a tee. As he kicks, the goal is to make the ball tumble end over end, not fly in a spiral. This tumbling effect creates more drag in the air than a ball flying nose first, so the tumbling ball will soar more steadily. This steadiness makes it possible for the kicker to be more accurate about making it go where he wants.

Passing the Football

When a quarterback passes a football, one of his goals is accuracy. He wants to make the football travel precisely to the spot where he thinks a receiver will arrive by the time the ball gets there. Another goal is to launch the ball with enough force and speed that a defensive player does not have time to run in and intercept it. In addition to the angle of the throw, the starting velocity and the force of gravity are important. This is because the faster something soars, the more space it will cover before gravity pulls it to the ground. The range the football will go can be calculated by an equation based on the laws of projectile motion. The equation figures in the velocity, the angle of launch, and the acceleration of the ball.

Players in a game do not have time to do the math, even if they wanted to. They make very fast judgments. They consider wind conditions. They quickly note where opponents are and where the receiver they are aiming for is heading.

Legendary Pittsburgh Steelers quarterback Terry Bradshaw drops back with the index finger of his throwing hand on the tip of the football in order to increase the speed of his pass.

Practice and experience make them experts at knowing how hard and at what angle to throw the ball to make it go where they want.

The typical player passes with an overhand or sideways movement and keeps his eye on the receiver the whole time. For the best control of a throw, a quarterback must keep his hand close to the ball's middle, which is its center of gravity. Yet to thrust with the greatest force, he needs to make his grip as far back on the ball as possible. Since he cannot do both, he holds the ball somewhere on the back half. Terry Bradshaw, a former quarterback with the Pittsburgh Steelers, had his own technique. He put his index (pointing finger) on the back tip of the ball, which increased the speed of his passes.

Just like a punt, forward passes can be tight, or they can be wobbly spins. The best throw is one that makes the football travel in a strong tight spiral. A player achieves this by throwing so that the ball rolls off his hand. His index finger should be the last part of his body touching the ball. Although gravity affects the path of the ball, it does not alter its spinning. This principle is called the conservation of angular momentum. The concept means that a rotating sphere will keep spinning at the same speed around the same axis unless acted on by an outside force, like a gust of wind. The faster the ball spins, the more steadiness it maintains in flight. Skillful passes spin at about 600 rotations per minute and can move 45 mph (72kph).

The Mischievous Magnus Effect

Another influence on spinning balls is the Magnus effect, a principle named after Heinrich Gustav Magnus (1802–1870). He was a German chemist and physicist, who first studied the effect in 1853 and did measurements on rotating balls. As a ball spins, air flows over it. On one side, the airflow goes in the same direction as the spin, so the air speeds up on that side. On the other side, however, the air flows in the opposite direction of the rotation, which causes the air to slow down. The slower air flow creates a greater pressure buildup and pushes the ball sideways. The Magnus effect is seen when a football spirals up in the air and then as it descends, it slips to one side near the end of its flight.

Throwing the football effectively is even harder when the player has to throw it on the run. A soaring, spinning football that veers to one side also requires quick and accurate calculations from the player trying to catch it.

CHAPTER 4

Catching and Running

There is a famous catch in football history that sent quarterback Joe Montana and his San Francisco 49ers to their first Super Bowl game. In 1981, San Francisco was about to lose a home game to the Dallas Cowboys. The score was 27-21 with only 51 seconds left. Montana caught the snap and sped to the right. Dwight Clark, a wide receiver, moved into the end zone at the far left side of the field, which put Montana in a dilemma. He was driving to the right, essentially facing the right side of the field. Clark, the only receiver he could pass to, stood downfield to his left. To throw to Clark, Montana had to twist his body around and throw backwards off the wrong foot. Quickly fine-tuning his pass on the run, Montana sent the ball sailing toward the end zone. Clark, who was more than six feet tall, leaped over a Dallas player and snatched the ball out of the air to score and win the game.

Plays like this well-known catch do not happen because of good luck. They happen because receivers and runners constantly make rapid-fire mental calculations about where the ball is going and where they need to be. Ball carriers also use their skills to gain speed, dodge the defense, and tightly hold the football after they catch it.

When a player throws to a receiver, the two players' thoughts might look on paper like two arrows. One arrow

The Wilson Pro Ball

Since 1941, the official football of the NFL has been the Wilson ball. It is the only ball used in all NFL regular season, playoff, and Pro Bowl games. The factory at Ada, Ohio, employs one hundred and fifty workers, and every year they make thousands of regulation footballs by hand from genuine leather hides. A special commemorative football is made for each Super Bowl.

Since 1941, the National Football League has used footballs manufactured by Wilson in all regular season, playoff, and Super Bowl games.

would start from the thrower's location, and the other arrow would start from the receiver's location. The two arrows would meet at the point where the receiver and ball come together. As a wide receiver for the Arizona Cardinals, Larry Fitzgerald amazes people when he plucks pass after pass out of the air. In photographs, he is seen making catches with his eyes closed. Yet Fitzgerald has said he does not fully understand his method himself.

Joan Vickers has some ideas about why he is so good at catching. She is a cognitive psychologist at the University of Calgary in Canada, who has researched the eye movements of athletes. She had the athletes wear special goggles with cameras that recorded their eye movements. What she learned helped her analyze Fitzgerald's techniques. She concluded that he has mastered two skills—the quiet eye and predictive control.

With the Click of an Eye

Vickers says no receiver sprinting downfield can easily focus on the football in flight. To track its pattern accurately, Vickers says players like Fitzgerald must quickly predict the ball's

movements long before the football descends. Sometimes their only chance to do this is right when the ball leaves the quarterback's hands. Instantly, they must assess its speed, direction, and rotation, and when and where it will come down. Vickers says that in order to judge the ball's movements correctly, the receiver uses the quiet eye method.

He uses his eyes like a camera. It is as if a player opens the shutter and snaps a mental picture with as long an exposure as he can manage. While on the run, the player accesses information from the mental picture and rapidly uses it to determine where he should go.

It seems as if Fitzgerald may be able to actually see the ball's destination in his mind and then position himself to be ready. This ability is called predictive control. The skill allows the player to collect information from the eyes and use it to foretell the ball's path. Vickers has noticed that the best hockey goalies and tennis players she has studied first use the quiet eye method to mentally snap and hold a clear picture of an approaching object. Then while the object is coming toward them, they do a rapid recall of similar snapshots in their memories. By recalling mental pictures of past plays, they quickly compare and figure precisely when the ball will come down and where they need to be. They can predict so well that many athletes make plays and catch with their eyes closed, as Fitzgerald does. Predictive control is what enables a receiver to run under the ball without looking at it, then to turn at just the right time and catch it.

From Rolling Pin to Pigskin

Fitzgerald gives credit for his visual skills to his grandfather, an optometrist, or eye doctor, in Chicago. When Fitzgerald was in the first grade, his granddad, Dr. Robert Johnson, created drills for him to do. Johnson understood that young students had to work their minds and hands in harmony in order to learn reading and writing skills. Holding a book while the eyes scan it and writing on paper require hand-eye coordination. He designed activities to improve Fitzgerald's hand-eye coordination. He also wanted to make sure his grandson learned which of his eyes was dominant, or which eye worked better than the other one.

A person's dominant eye processes information faster and offers a more accurate line of sight than the non-dominant eye. Athletes always know whether they are left-handed or right-handed, and it also helps them to know if their left or

The Eyes Have It

After the brain, the eyes are the most complex organs.

More than 2 million working parts make up the eyes.

Most people blink about 10,000 times daily.

Eyes handle 36,000 bits of data per hour.

The world sees only 1/6th of a person's eyeball.

The human eyeball weighs about .98 ounces (28g).

Eyes focus on about 50 things per second.

Human eyes can detect 500 shades of gray.

right eye is dominant. An athlete performs best by using his dominant eye in unison with his dominant hand and arm.

To develop these important skills, Johnson had Fitzgerald stand on balance beams and shaky boards. While balancing himself, Fitzgerald did hand-eye drills, like tracing the shapes of letters in the air. As Fitzgerald grew older, his grandfather customized the exercises for sports. One exercise had to do with a ball hanging from the ceiling. The seams of the ball were painted pink, and the ball had yellow and green dots on it. Fitzgerald used a rolling pin that had been painted with three stripes: one pink, one green, and one yellow. His job was to swing the pin like a bat and hit the ball, but not just any random way. He was supposed to aim so the green stripe on the rolling pin would hit the green spot on the ball. Likewise, he made the yellow stripe on the pin strike the yellow circle on the ball.

The ball rotated while it hung from the ceiling, so Fitzgerald was getting great practice at bringing together two masses that were both in motion. He was developing his brain's ability of predictive control. "People don't realize it, but we actually see with our brains,"[17] Johnson said in an interview with *The Wall Street Journal*. Fitzgerald has said his grandfather's training helped him become the player he is. Once a player like Fitzgerald has a good feel for where the ball is going, he can put his efforts into steaming ahead to reach it.

Running to the Max

Wide receivers like Fitzgerald usually reach the greatest speeds of all players, and this is due to the positions players take at the line of scrimmage. Wide receivers typically line up on the far left and far right of the other players, who are lined up closer to each other. The other players are also closer

University of Arkansas wide receiver Marqual Wade finds an open space along the sidelines in order to reach maximum speed while running for a touchdown.

to the center of the line of scrimmage, which means there are more defensive players nearby to block them once the ball is snapped. When a wide receiver takes off, he has fewer opposing players near him so he has more open space. An open field is needed for a player to accelerate and reach his maximum speed. In football, people refer to a player's average speed since someone running goes faster or slower over the span of the run. If someone says, "The receiver runs a 4-5 45," that means the player can run 45 yards in 4.5 seconds from a standing start. To get his average speed, the 45 yards is divided by the time, 4.5 seconds, to get 10 yards or 30 feet per second (9m/s).

The task of a running back is to move the football down the field fast using whatever means needed. Good receivers and running backs are able to spot holes among the bodies on the field and run through those open paths. While playing for the University of Hawaii, Mike Bass said, "I get the ball, for some reason I see holes. I'm not really sure how."[18] When a runner sees an opportunity to cut through a space and must change direction, he sets his foot down to stop his motion. His foot puts force against the turf. The force stops his current movement and pushes him off in another direction. This action demonstrates the idea of Newton's third law that for every action there is an equal but opposite reaction.

The other thing that helps stop him is the friction between his foot and the ground. Friction is the force that happens when two surfaces rub against one another and is an important element in changing direction. Friction enables a runner to alter his movement, but friction can also cause a player to get hurt.

Friction Is Friend and Foe

A wet field makes for less friction and big trouble. As a player clamps his foot on wet grass or turf, the water reduces the frictional force between his foot and the ground. It is more difficult for him to stop, so he may slide and tumble.

A player's cleat kicks up clumps of grass as he runs across the field. The friction created when a player's foot comes in contact with the ground his higher when the grass or turf is dry than when it is wet.

He can also fall if the ground is dry, and he pushes too hard when he puts his foot down. As his foot first makes contact with the ground, static friction comes into play. Once the runner's foot breaks away from the static grip and begins to slide, the factors of sliding friction take over. When a player moves, his foot pushes against the ground in the opposite direction he wants to run. The force required for his foot to breakaway from the turf has to do with the downward force being applied, and that force is usually the weight of the athlete. The larger the player, the larger the frictional forces on him.

The friction between a football shoe with cleats and the turf or grass is like friction between two pieces of Velcro hooked together. It takes a lot of force to make one piece of Velcro slide over the other because the hooks of each side are attached. When enough force is used to free that attachment, the force needed to slide the pieces is less. The moving force is less than the breakaway force. If the player does not slip or fall and dodges the opposition, he can charge through the open space he spotted. Yet more players are bound to race toward him, and he must get around them too.

Juking Around

A ball carrier usually cannot outrun all the opposing players. He must be quick and agile enough to avoid them. Power backs often use their mass to race straight up the field, plowing through those in their way. The quickest players

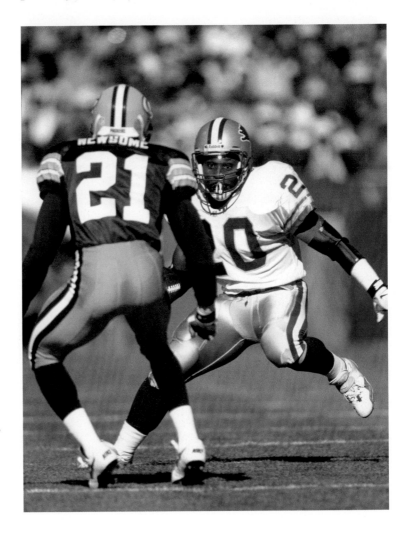

Detroit Lions running back Barry Sanders uses his quickness and agility in order to change directions mid-run and juke around other players.

tend to be those who are lighter weight and shorter. As they run up a field, they juke. Juking is making a quick change in direction, usually one after the other in which the player alters his speed.

Changing speed and direction rapidly requires big accelerations. It is a great skill for a receiver and running back

DRILLS

Changing speed and direction rapidly requires big accelerations. It is a great skill for a receiver and running back to have. Drills such as the one shown here help players learn to accelerate and decelerate quickly and to change directions without losing their footing.

to have. Just as a defender is about to collide with him, he switches his course lightning fast, even turning to go at a right angle from his previous direction. Since his opponent has nothing to hit, his momentum causes him to collapse on the ground. Barry Sanders, formerly of the Detroit Lions (1989–99), was famous for his juking skills.

While being pursued, a running back wants to keep the ball and gain as much yardage as he can. If opposing players cannot take him down, they will try to knock the ball from his grasp. A skilled player knows how to hold the ball so the defensive player cannot dislodge it.

Getting a Grip

To get a grip on the ball and keep it, a player should support the ball in four places. If carrying the ball on his right, he would wrap his fingers around the front tip. His forearm would squeeze on the right lower part of the ball to press it to his rib cage, which would support the opposite side of the ball on its upper left quarter. The bicep of the player's right arm would press and hold against the rear tip of the ball. A defensive player has to work hard to dislodge the ball when it is gripped in this way.

To break the ball free, the defender must make the football swivel around one of the four points where it is braced. He must also cause the angle of rotation to be great enough so the ball will pivot loose. He has to create angular acceleration. The acceleration will happen only if there is unbalanced torque or twisting on the ball. Torque causes objects to pivot or to rotate on an axis. If a defender applies force that causes the ball to swivel clockwise at one of the four points, the ball carrier has the advantage. He can apply force at the other three points to create torque that moves the ball in a counter-clockwise position. Then the sum of the forces applied is zero. There is no unbalanced torque taking affect, so the angular acceleration does not happen, and the carrier keeps his hold. Instead of trying to rotate the ball out of the carrier's grasp, the defender could try to push the ball straight out.

Whatever force the defender applies to an area of the ball, the carrier must counter with force from the pressure points to prevent any unbalanced torque dislodging the ball. A runner does his best to keep the ball, avoid the opposition, and run to the end zone, while the defensive players work just as hard to block him or bring him down.

CHAPTER 5

Blocking And Tackling

Vince Lombardi said, "Some people try to find things in this game that don't exist, but football is only two things—blocking and tackling."[19] Successful blocks and tackles enable a team's plays to work and cause the opposition to fail. What happens to two players who slam against each other depends on the natural laws that have to do with momentum, collisions, and force.

The word "momentum" is used a lot in sports and is often used incorrectly. In the middle of a game, the announcer might say, "The Dallas Cowboys have the momentum." Fans know that means the Cowboys have the edge; it feels like the game is going their way. Yet the term really belongs to physics and means "mass in motion."

Momentum

Newton called momentum "the quantity of motion." It has to do with a player's weight and how fast he is moving. This combination provides a player with the might to charge down the field through opposing players. Momentum (p) is figured by multiplying an object's mass (m) times its velocity (v), so $p = mv$. Mass is the amount of matter in an object, and the weight of a player is used for mass in equations for football

Since momentum is a product of mass and velocity, a lighter-weight player moving more quickly can have the same momentum of a heavier player running more slowly.

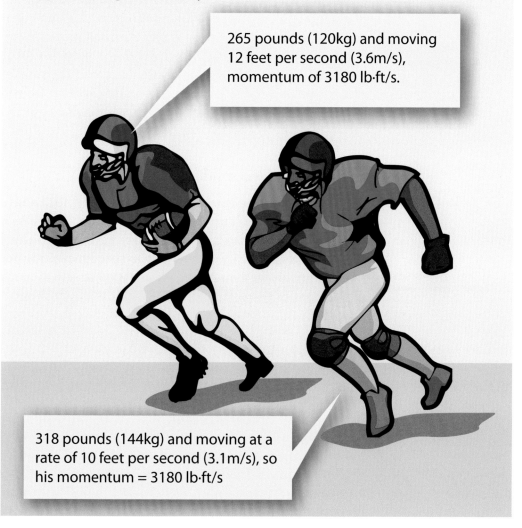

265 pounds (120kg) and moving 12 feet per second (3.6m/s), momentum of 3180 lb·ft/s.

318 pounds (144kg) and moving at a rate of 10 feet per second (3.1m/s), so his momentum = 3180 lb·ft/s

physics. Velocity is a combination of the speed the object is traveling and the direction it is going. If a linebacker's average speed is 10 feet per second (3.1m/s), and he is moving east, his velocity would be 10 feet per second (3.1m/s) to the east. If the linebacker weighed 318 pounds (144kg), his momentum would be figured like this:

p = mv
p = 318 lb (m) x 10 ft/s (v)
p = 3180 lb·ft/s eastward (1442kg)

Since it is a product of mass and velocity, the momentum of a lighter-weight player moving more quickly can equal the momentum of a heavier player running more slowly. A runner at 265 pounds (120kg) weighs 53 pounds (24kg) less than the 318-pound (144kg) linebacker. If the smaller runner moves faster at 12 feet per second (3.6m/s), he will have the same momentum as the bigger linebacker.

p = mv
p = 265 lb (m) x 12 ft/s (v)
p = 3180 lb·ft/s eastward (1442kg)

Players sprinting across the field do not typically have equal momentum. If runners have an open space in which to run, they can accelerate or increase their speed. Since speed is part of velocity, an increase in speed means greater momentum for the runner, and players want to gain as much momentum as possible before they tackle the opposition.

Big Body Hits

Blocks and tackles happen nonstop in a football game. Duffy Daugherty (1915–1987) was a player and coach who was inducted into the College Football Hall of Fame in 1984. According to Daugherty, "Football isn't a contact sport, it's a collision sport. Dancing is a contact sport."[20] It takes force to stop a runner. It is not just because he is strong and highly motivated to score. His body will be difficult to stop because it is mass moving on a path, and it will keep moving until some force makes it stop. It is the job of a lineman to do just that—apply force to stop a ball carrier.

A force applied to one side of an object but not the other will either speed the object up or slow it down. If a force pushes in the same direction as the motion of the object, then the force speeds the object up. This is easy to understand by

thinking of a lineman running behind a wide receiver in the same direction. When the lineman tackles the wide receiver, the receiver's speed is increased. This increase in speed may just last until he hits the ground or collides with more players, but he moves faster for a few seconds. The opposite is also true. When a force pushes opposite the motion of the mass, it slows the object down. Linemen hunker down and face each other before each play. The defensive lineman's job is to stop the other team from advancing. When he blocks an opposing player head-on, he applies force to the player

A defender moves the mass of his body in the opposite direction of the ball carrier in order to change his momentum and thus slow down or stop his opponent's advance.

in the opposite direction of the player's motion and slows him down, often enough to stop him. Whether a force acts in the same or opposite direction of an object, the force will change the velocity of an object. And if the velocity of the object is changed, the momentum of the object is also changed.

A tackle alters the momentum of the man who is tackled and of the one who does the tackling. Whatever momentum one player loses in a block or tackle, the other man gains. The total momentum of two bodies that collide remains the same before and after the contact. No momentum is lost. This law is called conservation of momentum, and it means that momentum is always maintained or kept constant in collisions.

If a player running with the ball and the player tackling him have equal momentum, the motion of the two will stop when they impact. Otherwise, the player with the greater momentum fares better. If the player running with the ball has more momentum than the tackler, he will knock the tackler away. The tackler will be thrust backwards with a momentum equal to the difference between the two players. Likewise, if the ball carrier has less momentum than the tackler, he will be knocked away—with a momentum equal to the difference between the two players. Adrian Wilson, a safety in the NFL for the Arizona Cardinals, said, "It's all about timing and the leverage you've got to have once you make impact, so the other player goes back, and not you."[21]

Bouncy or Not Bouncy

Massive players crashing together results in two kinds of collisions: elastic and inelastic. In an elastic collision, players do not stay in contact after they hit. Their bodies separate like two billiard, or pool, balls bouncing off each other. When the two masses stay together and move as one, the collision is called inelastic. In an elastic collision, two things are kept

Energy Never Goes Away

The word energy comes from the Greek word energeia, which means "being at work." Most types of energy are either a form of kinetic energy or potential energy.

Kinetic energy is the energy an object has because of its movement, like a train moving. Potential energy is energy that is stored and available for use, like a lifted arm holding a hammer. Energy can be changed from one kind to another. In lightning, electric potential energy converts into light, heat, and sound energy. The law of conservation of energy states that energy can be changed, but energy cannot be destroyed, and new energy cannot be created.

constant or conserved. One is momentum and the other is kinetic energy, which is an object's ability to do work on something else. The force that one player hits another player with increases the kinetic energy of the person being hit. Kinetic energy is based on the force of the impact times the distance over which it was applied. What happens to the kinetic energy depends on what kind of collision occurs.

A fullback and a linebacker may slam together in midair, hold on to each other, and travel together (inelastic collision). The speed at which they move together is reduced because the difference in momentum is now spread over the combined mass of the two players. In a totally inelastic crash-up, momentum is conserved, but kinetic energy is not. No kinetic energy is lost, but some of it is reshuffled. When one helmet whacks another and shoulder pads rub tightly together, kinetic energy gets transferred. These actions cause the atoms that make up the men and the materials on them to speed up. Air molecules move and produce snapping, cracking, and swooshing sounds, and molecules in the uniforms chafing together move faster and make heat. The number of atoms that existed before the collision is the same number of atoms that exists after, but some of the kinetic energy has been reorganized into sound and heat.

The natural laws of motion maintain a balance of momentum and energy when two players pit their 300-pound masses against each other on the football field. Still, nothing takes away the pain and punch of enormous body slams.

How Hard is Hard?

Everyday people's bodies bear the forces that come with routine activities such as walking, but football players endure forces that are far greater than what the average person experiences. All mass in motion results in an increase in g-force, which is the force of gravity on the acceleration of a body. On a spaceship where the atmosphere is weightless, the g-force of an object is zero. A race car speeding around a turn on a track exerts a g-force of about 5.3. Riding a rollercoaster puts about 5 gs of force on a body, or five times the normal force of gravity. A pounding on the football field can reach a g-force of 150, thirty times higher than the force felt on a rollercoaster. Ronald Wolfley played for the St. Louis/Arizona Cardinals from 1985 to 1991. He once hit a linebacker so hard that Wolfley knocked himself out. Minutes later he was right back in the game. Then he did it again—knocked himself unconscious once more with another body slam.

Dr. Timothy Gay is a physics professor at the University of Nebraska and the author of *The Physics of Football*. In his

Legendary Chicago Bears linebacker Dick Butkus, playing in a 1972 game, hits Green Bay Packers running back John Brockington with such force that it flips Brockington over his shoulder.

book, he calculates the force that Dick Butkus used when he brought down a ball carrier. Dick Butkus played for the Chicago Bears (1965–1973) and became a member of the Pro Football Hall of Fame in 1979. He is said to be one of the best linebackers of his generation. To calculate the force of Butkus's hits, Gay uses the equation in Newton's second law: Force equals mass times acceleration (F = ma).

Gay explains that the force Butkus applied to his opponent is directly related to or proportional to his opponent's mass times his acceleration. Gay puts the opponent's weight at 245 pounds (111kg), which is about equal to Butkus's weight. He begins to calculate the acceleration (a) by first figuring the running back's initial speed as 30 feet per second (9m/s). Then after Butkus hit him, the player stopped cold, and his speed was zero. Gay watched a slow-motion replay to determine the duration of the hit. From the initial contact to when the running back stopped moving forward was two-tenths of a second. To get acceleration, he divides the change in speed by the time span. He actually figures deceleration because the runner was stopped in his tracks. The deceleration is indicated by a minus sign in the equation.

A simple version of Gay's calculations looks like:

$a = (0 \text{ ft/s} - 30 \text{ ft/s}) / 0.2 \text{ s} = -150$ feet per second squared

$F = ma$

$m = 245$ lbm (111kg)

$a = -150 \text{ ft/s}^2 \ (-45.72 \text{m/s}^2)$

Then he uses a force equations calculator and gets a result of:

$F =$ about 1142.2 pound force (518kgf).

According to Gay, when Butkus slammed his opponents, it was as if a small killer whale had hit them with about three-fifths of a ton of force. Players stopped by Butkus probably did not forget the impact. Jim Brown wanted players who tackled him to remember the experience. Brown played as a running back for the Cleveland Browns and is considered one of the greatest American pro athletes of all time. He once told Baltimore Colts tight end John Mackey, "Make sure when anyone tackles you he remembers how much it hurts."[22]

Tackling With Torque

Linemen need momentum to topple an opponent. Momentum is a product of mass times velocity, and since linemen do not have open running space available, they are not able to greatly increase their velocity. So massive weight is a big advantage when they are trying to take another player to the ground. Their mass increases their momentum. It also helps them stand strong against a tackle, since as Newton wrote in his second law, the more mass an object has, the harder it is to move. Size matters in a football game, but coaches teach their tacklers methods based on the laws of gravity and torque that can take down even the biggest men.

Tampa Bay Buccaneers running back Michael Pittman is lifted off of his feet by the torque created by a low hit from the Atlanta Falcons defense.

A low point on the body is the best place for one player to tackle another. The attacker wants to avoid the player's center of mass or gravity, which is where all the body mass is focused or is concentrated in strength. A man's center of mass is just above his navel, while a woman's center is located lower, nearer her hip area. When tackled low on the body, below the center of mass, the runner's feet turn or rotate in the air in the same direction as the tackle. This rotation or movement is due to torque.

Two factors make up torque: the total force used multiplied by the distance the force is placed from the center of mass. When a tackler hits another player right at the center of mass, the player does not turn or rotate. Striking low on the body allows tacklers to use less of their energy and strength and to be more likely to turn and move another player. Coaches also teach players to keep pumping their legs on the turf when they tackle. This creates more force and gives them better balance. A lineman usually stays in a crouching position to make it harder for another player to hit him low. A tackler is forced to hit him higher and nearer his center of mass, which means he will not rotate and will be harder to move. Defensive linemen know how important it is to not get tackled when they are protecting their own goal in the last 10 yards (9m) before the goal line.

Ronald Wolfley, the player who knocked himself out twice, once said, "There's no feeling like running down the field as fast as you can. You hear all these horrible grunts and slams and bangs. Bodies are flying and feet are stomping. Then you find the guy with the ball … and knock his brains out."[23]

Knocking someone's brains out is not a law of physics. It is a reaction to playing the game with the might needed to win. Even though amazing athletic feats are controlled by the laws of physics, players use instinct and experience to perform. Yet understanding the natural laws at work in the game of football makes the sport more fun to watch and participate in. It also has brought about a better understanding of how to protect players.

CHAPTER 6

Staying in the Game: Nutrition, Equipment, and Injuries

P layers in the NFL tackle each other about 100 times per game. Their bodies take pounding after pounding that rattle their teeth and jar their bones, and they must be able to endure almost an hour of hard playing. Players need to be in top shape in order to play their best, and physical training is one way coaches and trainers prepare and take care of football players. Yet a good football program covers a range of health concerns—from what players should eat and what they should avoid to protective body gear and injury prevention and treatment.

An ideal diet for a football player is one that improves his total health as well as his game performance. Football trainers and sports nutritionists plan a player's diet around what he needs to play his position well—whether a player needs to gain weight, lose weight or body fat, and build muscle mass. The average NFL player weighs about 250 pounds (113kg), although many players weigh more than 300 pounds (136kg).

Pittsburgh Steelers offensive lineman Ramon Foster blocks ahead of wide receiver Hines Ward in a game in 2010. Lineman use their large size to stop opposing players or clear paths for smaller, speedier teammates.

Troy Hatton at the University of New Mexico says, "Offensive and defensive lineman require the most weight. These are our front men. They are in the trenches protecting the quarterback or trying to get to the opposing teams quarterback."[24] The heaviest player on his team is a defensive lineman who weighs 350 pounds (158kg), while the lightest player is a wide receiver weighing in at 140 pounds (63kg). "The skill positions, defensive backs and wide receivers," he continues, "are positions that require speed, and generally those players would not carry any extra weight."[25]

While the average man in the United States eats between 2,600 and 3,500 calories a day, NFL athletes take in between 5,000 and 10,000 calories daily during training camps. Some players need as many as 9,000 calories daily, which is equal to eating about thirty hamburgers in one day. If a coach wants a player to lose weight, the man must burn off more calories than he consumes. Usually receivers and defensive backs eat less during the off-season in order to keep their weight as it is or to lose pounds. If a player needs to gain weight, he must consume more calories in a day than he burns off. Each player can burn 2,000 to 3,000 calories on the field during the two daily practice sessions. Linemen often consume 1,500 calories more than their teammates each day during training camps in order to maintain their size. The players' diets are based on how many grams of carbohydrates, protein, and fats they need daily for each pound of their body weight.

Catering staff tend to a buffet prepared for Baltimore Ravens players during training camp. Nutritionists monitor what players eat before and during the playing season to ensure that their diets are healthful and provide sufficient amounts of protein.

Camp Food

While at camp, athletes practice into the night and need a lot of fuel. Camp cooks lay out huge spreads of food for meals and provide snacks and even a late night buffet. In the first week of camp, a chef can cook 2,000 pounds (907kg) of chicken, 300 pounds (136kg) of lean steak, and more than 400 pounds (181kg) of potatoes. Pizza, burgers, burritos, and desserts are available in their wholesome forms. A healthy diet is recommended for players no matter what the season, but during training camp, nutritionists forbid empty calories. Those are calories from foods that do not provide any nutritional benefit. French fries and onion rings are delicious, but players are told to avoid fried foods during training preseason and in-season. Even though training camps offer all-you-can-eat

buffets, nutritionists make sure the foods offered use healthy ingredients like lean meats, fish, lowfat dairy products, eggs, soy, canola and olive oils, and nuts.

They also make sure there are plenty of foods with high carbohydrate (or carb) content like whole grain breads and cereals, fruits, and vegetables. The football player's demanding training program increases his body's ability to store carbohydrates in muscle. Carbs are the body's main form of energy. When carbohydrates are eaten and digested, the carbs that are not needed right away are stored in the body as glycogen. Later, the glycogen is changed into glucose, which supplies energy when it is broken down by the body.

Dave Binder has his players follow a high protein, high carbohydrate diet and says, "We often supplement their diets with protein shakes."[26] Protein is found mainly in animal products like meats, fish, eggs, and dairy foods. It is converted into glycogen much more slowly than carbs, so it is not a ready source of energy. Yet it exists in every cell of the body, which uses it to build and mend tissues. Protein helps the body make hormones and chemicals that are necessary for good health and builds strong bones, blood, skin, and muscles.

Muscle Meals

In 2006 Jamie Bellavance wrote an article for *Men's Health* magazine called "The NFL's Secret Muscle Foods." In it he says that people should treat their bodies like a business and do what makes it operate the best. They should not take in foods just because they taste good, but because they do a job. A food's job may be to hydrate, repair muscle, prevent muscle cramping, or to restore minerals and vitamins that the body sweats out. Bellavance lists eleven foods and drinks that NFL players eat to build lean muscle. Eggs are especially good for building muscles, immunity, and good vision. Waffles are good fuel for the heart muscle. Fruits and

New York Jets linebacker Jamaal Westerman takes a water break during warm-ups before a game in 2009. In addition to following a healthful diet, football players must stay properly hydrated during games in order to perform at their best.

vegetables provide the body with liquids, and vegetables help mend muscles. Milk strengthens bones and helps with muscle contractions. In addition to creating lean muscle, chicken breasts are helpful in providing energy and strengthening memory. Fish not only aids in soothing joint irritation, it repairs muscles and makes the immune system stronger. Pasta and rice give energy and speed recovery after exercise. The last secret muscle food on Bellavance's list are sports drinks, which give the body the liquid it needs and prevent muscle cramping.

It is especially important for athletes to take in plenty of liquids to avoid dehydration, which means the body lacks enough fluid to keep working properly. Dehydration is dangerous for anyone. Players need at least 16 ounces of water or of sport drinks two hours before playing and should drink one or the other at every break and during half time. On a hot day, the weight of the uniform and equipment makes the body hotter. A football player can sweat off one gallon (3.8L) of water in a game or practice. Illness from heat occurs most often during the first few days of preseason practice as players are adjusting to constant training conditions.

The Body Craves Water

The human body is at least 60 percent water, which makes is possible for the body to control body temperature and to provide a way for nutrients to get to organs. Since each molecule of water has two hydrogen atoms and one oxygen atom, water carries oxygen to cells. It also removes waste and protects joints and organs. People lose water when they urinate, perspire, breathe, and exercise, so it must be replaced often. Just how much water do people need? One way to know is to figure someone's body weight in pounds and divide that by two. If a girl weighs 110 pounds (49kg), she needs 55 ounces of water each day. She could get that by drinking seven medium-size glasses of water. Someone who exercises should drink another eight ounces of water for every twenty minutes they work out.

Professional football players are expected to take maintaining their health seriously, and it is also a player's responsibility to know what substances are banned by the league and avoid them.

Just Say, "No."

In 1987 the NFL established drug guidelines for its players, and the policy is stricter than those for baseball and hockey professionals. The rules state that a player can be suspended if he tests positive for banned substances, and some players have been suspended without pay for up to four games. Several dozen substances appear on the banned list, including anabolic-androgenic steroids, growth hormones, and diuretics.

Anabolic-androgenic steroids are manmade substances that are similar to natural hormones in the body. Steroids speed up the growth of skeletal muscle and increase the development of adult male traits. Some athletes use steroids to increase strength and to enhance or improve physical performance. However, their use can cause many physical and psychological problems like tumors of the liver and kidneys, mood swings, and violent behavior. Steroids are banned both for health reasons and because their use gives a player an unfair advantage.

Although the National Football League has strict guidelines that prohibit the use of steroids, growth hormones, and other drugs, some players have used these banned substances as a way of getting a competitive edge.

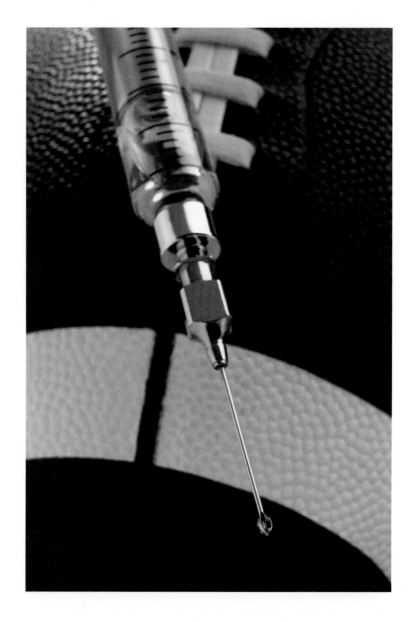

Another substance banned by the NFL is human growth hormone (HGH). Human growth hormone is a natural substance produced by the pituitary gland. It causes the human body to grow and mature normally. Doctors use a synthetically produced version of HGH called rHGH to treat growth disorders in children and a serious lack of energy in older people. Some athletes also take the hormone to enlarge their muscles and boost their performance in sports, even though the drug is not approved for this use. When a doctor supervises its use, the hormone can be used safely, but misuse has resulted in heart problems, liver and thyroid damage, diabetic coma, and even death.

Diuretics are drugs that doctors prescribe to control high blood pressure and other disorders. They increase the amount of urine the body produces and rid the body of too much fluid. Some athletes in sports like horse racing and rowing use them to make sure they do not weigh more than the limit for a certain category. Typically, football players do not use diuretics, but some players have taken them in order to hide their use of steroids. Because diuretics make people urinate more often, the urine checked in a drug test may be weak enough that steroid use will not be detected. Using these drugs improperly can result in dehydration, loss of coordination and balance, muscle cramps, and an irregular heartbeat.

Food supplements used by athletes sometimes contain banned substances. Creatine is muscle fuel that occurs naturally in meat and fish. It is extracted from these foods and sold as a diet supplement that is advertised as having the ability to pump up muscles. Although the NFL has not banned creatine, some of the forms it is sold in contain banned substances. Creatine can be dangerous if overused, causing dehydration and kidney problems.

The NFL conducts random testing of players for banned substances throughout the year. The 2010-11 season began with sixteen suspensions for use of banned substances—nine of those players were caught using performance enhancing drugs. Seven men were suspended for substance abuse, which includes the use of illegal drugs and the misuse of prescription drugs, over-the-counter drugs, and alcohol.

Athletes have a personal responsibility to avoid harmful substances, stay healthy, and be ready to play in prime physical condition. They further protect themselves by wearing several pounds of gear to buffer the pounding they take on the field.

Hits to the Head

Since the mid-1800s, the number of collisions and tackles in football has risen because more people play in more games. Yet the number of major injuries has not increased very much. According to Dr. Timothy Gay, "This is primarily the result of increased kinetic energy being countered by dramatic improvements in the design and materials used in protective equipment."[27] In 1870 football players certainly did not have the kind of equipment that is standard today. They wore uniforms made of canvas, leather helmets with no face guards, and leather padding to shield other body parts. Modern helmets and other football equipment are designed to protect players by absorbing and spreading out shocks to the body.

The helmet is the most important piece of football gear. A players head is at risk of injury from hitting the ground or from crashing into other players. Helmet to helmet impacts during a game can snap a player's head back like a ragdoll's. According to Jim Harbaugh, who played seven seasons for the Chicago Bears, "You're kind of numb after 50 shots to the head."[28] When one head slams into another, the hit may only last a tenth of a second, but the force can be as much

Head-Harness

The first football helmet was made by a shoemaker in Annapolis, Maryland, in 1893. He made it for Admiral Joseph Mason Reeves, whose doctor had told him another blow to the head would kill him or make him insane. Three years later, George Barclay, a halfback for Lafayette College, decided to protect his ears and paid a harness maker to construct his design. It stayed on his head by means of three heavy leather straps, which is why the first football helmets came to be called head-harnesses. Padded leather helmets became mandatory in the 1930s. The modern hard plastic helmet was created by Paul Brown. It has a hard plastic top with thick padding on the inside, a facemask with one or more plastic or metal bars, and a chinstrap. Each position has a different kind of face mask to give the protection and visibility needed.

PROTECTIVE GEAR

Helmets and shoulder pads rank as the two most important pieces of protective gear. Both work by spreading the force of the impact widely over the surface of the player's head or body. The padding compresses or squeezes together when struck and increases the length of the blow over time, lessening the average force of it.

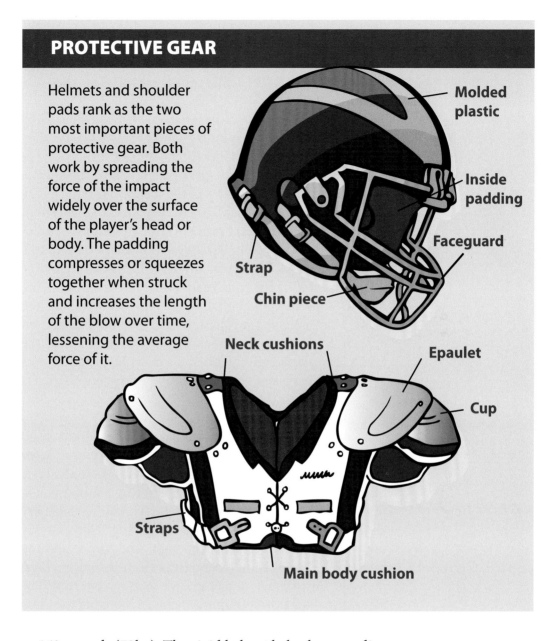

Molded plastic

Inside padding

Faceguard

Strap

Chin piece

Neck cushions

Epaulet

Cup

Straps

Main body cushion

as 160 pounds (72kg). The rigid helmet helps by spreading the force of the impact widely over the surface. If the helmet was flexible enough to be dented in where a head butt occurs, the pressure on the point of impact would be much greater. The standard football helmet is made of molded plastic with a foam rubber lining or an air-filled lining, in which air can be let in or out of for a perfect fit. A jolt makes the inside of the helmet move toward the head, and as the lining and head meet, the padding compresses or squeezes together. This takes more time than if there was no lining, and the increase in the length of the blow lessens the average force of it.

Mouth guards and facemasks are also vital for guarding the head area. Since the mouth guards are rigid plastic, they do not stretch out the duration of the impact as the lining of a helmet does. Instead, they spread out the force. That way a hit to the mouth is shared by all the teeth, so serious injury to one or several teeth is less likely. A facemask shields both mouth and face with bars made of strong plastic or plastic-coated steel. While some kickers and punters wear masks that have a single bar across the face, linemen often wear a cage-like mask. The cage keeps a player's face from being hit and stops an opponent's hand from reaching inside the mask. Most receivers and quarterbacks want the area in front of their eyes free, so their masks do not have bars near the eyes. Clear plastic face shields and sunshades are additional equipment that players can use. Another extra is a cap that is added to the outside of helmets for more protection against head slams.

According to critics, the standard helmet does a good job of preventing cuts and fractures, but it does little to guard against concussions and sub-concussions. Testing and certifications of helmets is done by a group that is funded by the manufacturers of helmets. Many people say an independent board should do the testing. They also say the testing has not been strict enough. The NFL is pushing for reform. In 2011, representatives from helmet makers, the NFL, the military, and NASCAR met in New York City. They discussed how to improve helmets. Some of the ideas include more shock absorbent padding, stronger chin straps, face masks designed to disperse shock better, and helmets that are suited to children's bodies. Helmets for children have been identical to those for adults, just smaller. Yet the padding inside helmets has always been made to absorb the force of an adult head. A child's head hits with less force, so when it contacts the lining, the padding does not compress as it should. The experts in New York City recommended that helmets be custom built for smaller heads. The main goal of the helmet summit was to bring about the development of head gear that does a better job of guarding against concussions for players of all ages.

Blows to the Body

While the helmet is the most crucial piece of football gear, shoulder pads rank second in importance. Shoulder and other body pads have evolved through the decades into high-tech armor. The leather shoulder pads that players wore in the 1920s were heavier than those worn today, but they were not designed to absorb shock. Modern shoulder pads and other body pads have a rigid plastic shell over shock absorbing foam materials. Players can lace shoulder pads tighter or looser to fit their bodies. The gear is one piece that protects the shoulders and the sternum or breastplate. Some kinds also cover the top of the arms and the rotator cuffs. Rib protectors or flak jackets are worn by some quarterbacks since they constantly expose their rib cages when they lift their arms to throw. Other types of pads are custom-made to protect the hips, thighs, knees, tailbones, and spines. Body padding works the same way that the lining inside a helmet does. The padding makes the collision time longer so the average force of a blow is lessened.

Performance Enhancing Gear

Some equipment not only offers protection but also improves the player's performance. A number of quarterbacks use gloves for better grip and control of the ball, and some just wear one glove on the throwing hand. Others refuse to wear them, saying they can pass more accurately with a bare hand that can feel the football. Receivers wear them the most since it is their job to catch the ball. Even though gels or other sticky materials cannot be applied to football gloves, the outside surfaces are made of

EXTRA POINT

Artificial turf is called "Astroturf" because it was first used at the Houston Astrodome in 1965.

a natural tacky material. Gloves warm a player's hands in cold weather and are vented for air flow on hot days. Linemen wear thickly-padded gloves that protect their fingers when they get caught in an opponent's face mask or get trampled on.

Players also wear special shoes. The type of shoes a player wears depends on the position he plays, the weather, and if the field is natural grass or artificial turf. Cleats that are 1/2 inches long (1.3cm) provide the best traction on dry fields. Wet grass fields require a longer cleat, like 3/8 inches (1cm) or 1 inch long (2.5cm). A typical choice for playing on artificial turf are shoes that have dozens of 1/2 inch long (1.3cm) cleats made of rubber. Larger players often wear shoes with more cleats than those worn by running backs and receivers. During warm-up, players try shoes with various lengths of cleats to find which will work the best. Many football boots have cleats that come off and can be exchanged for shorter or longer cleats, which are removed and put on with a power drill. That way a player can adjust his shoes to give the best traction based on the playing conditions for that game and field.

Wearing good gear and adjusting it for the weather and the playing field go a long way toward avoiding injuries. Still, bad things will always happen in an action-filled game like football and players are injured.

A Big Pain

Head injuries happen so often in football that Jim Murray (1919–1998), a sportswriter for the *Los Angeles Times*, wrote in one of his columns, "What about football? Is it a sport or a concussion?"[29] If a player leads with his helmet as he leaps into another, he can land a direct hit to the opponent's head. This could leave either or both players with a concussion, a jarring of the brain which is usually followed by loss of consciousness. A series of lesser hits to the head can cause a sub-concussion and eventually result in concussion-like problems: headache, vomiting, dizziness, lack of balance, short term memory loss, confusion, and being irritable.

Some football players say it is natural to lead with the head when going for a tackle, but the National Collegiate

A Career as a Certified Athletic Trainer (ACT)

To train as an ACT, students complete a program that is accredited by the Commission on Accreditation of Athletic Training (CAATE). The course work includes studies in anatomy and physiology, physics, exercise physiology, injury evaluation, rehabilitation, nutrition, risk management, and healthcare administration. Clinical practice is also required, and many students fulfill this by assisting the athletic trainer for a school's athletic team. They work under the supervision of an ACT. Once a student has graduated from training, he or she must pass the NATA's (National Athletic Trainer's Association) Board of Certification exam. It evaluates their knowledge of injury prevention, clinical evaluation, immediate care, treatment and rehabilitation, organization and administration, and professional responsibility. Certified trainers must also be licensed by the states in which they practice and must maintain their certification with classes that help them stay current in their field. More than seventy percent of ACTs go on to earn master's degrees, and many earn doctorial degrees.

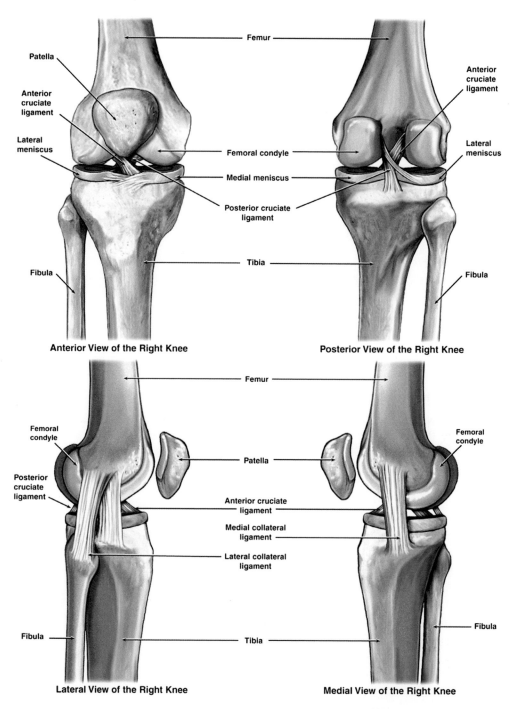

Anterior View of the Right Knee

- Femur
- Patella
- Anterior cruciate ligament
- Lateral meniscus
- Femoral condyle
- Medial meniscus
- Posterior cruciate ligament
- Tibia
- Fibula

Posterior View of the Right Knee

- Femur
- Anterior cruciate ligament
- Lateral meniscus
- Fibula

Lateral View of the Right Knee

- Femur
- Femoral condyle
- Posterior cruciate ligament
- Fibula
- Tibia

Medial View of the Right Knee

- Femoral condyle
- Patella
- Anterior cruciate ligament
- Medial collateral ligament
- Lateral collateral ligament
- Fibula

The "unhappy triad" is a common injury for football players. It happens when a hit strikes the knee and damages the ACL, MCL, and the medial meniscus.

Athletic Association outlawed all helmet-to-helmet contact, even if it is accidental. The rule states that no player shall initiate contact and target an opponent with the crown of his helmet. The NFL has tried to stop dangerous helmet-to-helmet hits, but they continue to occur. Mike Pereira was once an NFL official and is now a sports analyst. He wrote on FOXSports.com, "I am really bothered by the number of helmet-to-helmet hits … and the subsequent concussions that were caused as a result of those hits. Some of them were legal, and some were unavoidable. But, plain and simple, they are cheap shots, and the league needs to deal with this immediately."[30]

Another serious risk that football players face is spinal injuries. The spinal cord carries nerve signals from the brain to the rest of the body, so damage to it is very serious. Contact sports cause 10 percent of all spinal cord injuries in America due to impacts like hard body hits and falling. Patients with such damage may have decreased strength and coordination, as well as numbness for a long time. They could also permanently lose the function of their arms and/or legs.

Brain and spinal cord injuries are among the most serious that players face, but they are not the most common injuries. Dave Binder is the Head Athletics Trainer for football players at the University of New Mexico. He says that the three most common injuries are damage to the knee, ankle, and the shoulder. Fractures of the fingers, wrists, and legs make up about one-fourth of football injuries. As added protection against sprains and dislocations, players wrap tape around ankle, wrist, and knee joints.

Tackles can cause a fracture of the hip pointer, which is the bone that can be felt on each side near the waist. The "unhappy triad" is another common problem. It happens when a slam strikes the knee on the outside and leaves damage in three areas—to the two major ligaments and the medial meniscus, the strong cartilage on the inside of the knee. E.J. Holub, former linebacker for the Kansas City Chiefs, has had twelve knee operations to fix this kind of injury. Tackles also result in thigh injuries. When one player pounces and his helmet or shoulder pads ram into the other player's thighs, it can cause bruising, swelling, and bleeding.

An impaired knee, arm, shoulder, neck, or back once meant that an athlete's football career was over. Today that is not the case. Over the past thirty years, doctors have made great advances in treating sports-related problems. Doctors now replace a torn ligament with a tendon taken from somewhere else in the player's body. They successfully treat and rehabilitate athletes who have experienced spinal damage, concussions, and joint injuries. The athletes often go back on the field ready to blaze to victory in another big game.

CHAPTER **7**

A Winning Mindset: Playing the Psychological Game

Learning the skills of football is absolutely necessary for winning games, but there are more factors involved in a player and a team becoming successful. These factors cannot be measured like a runner's speed or the force of a tackle. They are mental attitudes and beliefs that shape how a player performs. Through the ages, experts have studied what separates those who reach their goals from those who do not. They have found common traits that are shared by athletes who repeatedly triumph.

Outstanding football players have a high level of confidence, a belief in their ability and their team's ability to perform well, and a focus so strong that they enter a zone of peak performance. They are also able to deal with setbacks. Mental training is now recognized as a powerful tool to take an athlete's performance to its highest level.

Peak Performance

Dr. Patrick Cohn is a master mental-game coach with a Ph.D. in applied sports psychology, which is the science and study of the mind as it relates to sports. Today he is the founder of Peak Performance Sports in Orlando, Florida. He works with football players to teach them to believe as individuals that they can succeed and that the game is winnable no matter who the opposing team is. He teaches them that once they have learned the art of football, they must have confidence

Legendary New York Jets quarterback Joe Namath drops back for a pass in the early 1970s. Namath's extreme confidence in his own abilities led him to make a famous statement guaranteeing his team would defeat the Miami Dolphins in the Super Bowl in 1969.

in the expertise they have acquired. It is not just a matter of having overall playing confidence. They must believe they can successfully carry out every needed play—passing, running, blocking, tackling, and kicking.

EXTRA POINT

Johnny Unitas was voted the league's best player when the NFL celebrated its first 50 years.

Dr. Cohn tells athletes to review the reasons their success is possible. These reasons may be past successes on the field, a good team and coach, a player's top physical condition, and numerous practice sessions. Johnny Unitas, one of the best NFL quarterbacks of all time, said, "There is a difference between conceit and confidence. Conceit is bragging about yourself. Confidence means you believe you can get the job done."[31] Joe Namath, a Hall of Fame quarterback, shared this view. He once said, "I've got news for you. We're gonna win the game. I guarantee it."[32]

Instead of thinking that another team is likely to beat them, Dr. Cohn instructs players to tell themselves over and over that their team is better than any they will play. He warns them not to allow misgivings because doubts are not helpful. Terry Bradshaw was a star quarterback for the Pittsburgh Steelers. He said, "What's the worst thing that can happen to a quarterback? He loses his confidence."[33]

When things go wrong, players must have patience, which Dr. Cohn says is a kind of confidence. A patient player reminds himself that his next play will be better and make a positive difference in the game. Whether on the field or off, players must keep this mindset of success. Ken Simonton, former NFL running back, put it this way. "Hey, we're like soldiers. Would you go to the Roman army and ask them if they thought they were going to win the battle? If I didn't think we could win, I wouldn't be here. I'd stay home and get fat."[34]

Zoning In and Out

Athletes and trainers talk about accessing "the zone" or being "in the zone." It is the mental condition that enables athletes to achieve to the peak of their abilities. When a player gets in the zone, his or her performance flows smoothly and easily. They execute perfect plays without having to think too hard about their moves. It is as if their subconscious is guiding them. In the zone, an athlete feels he or she cannot fail. A football player in the zone sees the ball early and knows exactly what play is needed next.

Lawrence Taylor, a Hall of Fame former linebacker for the New York Giants, said, "There were probably about five games in my career where everything was moving in slow motion and you could be out there all day, totally in the zone, and you don't even know where you are on the field, everything is just totally blocked out."[35]

The subconscious is the body's command center. For a football player, this means it is where his football instincts reside, where his football memories and experience can be retrieved. When players allow worry to take over, they cannot make plays calmly and easily. Panic freezes their best efforts. The conscious mind guides in a step by step way. In

In or Out of the Zone?

Jay P. Granat, Ph.D., has coached athletes and their families from every sport around the world. He has come up with some attitude statements for athletes. How they answer reveals whether they are playing in the zone.

"Yes" to the following statements means an athlete is not in the zone.

> Players I should beat are beating me.
> I cannot calm down and focus.
> My confidence is gone.
> Opponents intimidate me.

"Yes" to the following statements means an athlete performs in the zone.

> The game was a breeze.
> I did not think about anything.
> It felt magical.
> I was right on the ball.

contrast, the subconscious guides spontaneously based on experience and memory of what to do and how to do it.

Whether it is called confidence or being "in the zone," coaches have worked to instill a winning attitude in their players since football began.

Winning Words from Famous Coaches

The team's coach plays an important role in establishing a positive mindset and keeping the players motivated throughout every game. Vince Lombardi coached the Green Bay Packers and the Washington Redskins. He said, "Winning is not a sometime thing; it's an all the time thing. You don't win once in a while; you don't do things right once in a while; you do them right all of the time. Winning is a habit. Unfortunately, so is losing."[36] He taught that every time a football player goes out on the field, every inch of him must play, from his feet to his brain. Some guys just play with their heads, Lombardi said. He taught his men to also play with their hearts. He claimed that if he had a guy with a lot of heart and lot of head, the player would never come off the field second. He also said, "If it doesn't matter who wins or loses, then why do they keep score?"[37]

Tom Landry (1924–2000) is another legendary coach who led the Dallas Cowboys from the time they were founded in

Green Bay Packers coach Vince Lombardi is carried off the field by his players after a victory. Much of Lombardi's success as a coach came from his ability to motivate his team.

Tom Landry

During his time with the Giants, Tom Landry, at age 29, became a player-coach in charge of the defense. His degree in mechanical engineering inspired him to develop the flex defense. It was a four-man defensive line with three linebackers behind. It became such a success that most teams started using the system. Later when Landry coached the Dallas Cowboys, other teams used the flex defense against the Cowboys, so Landry devised the multiple offense to counter it. In the multiple offense, the linemen would head to the line of scrimmage and set down, then stand and hide behind other players who were rapidly switching positions. The opposing team did not know who was in what position. Both the flex defense and the multiple offense are standard practices for football teams from Pee Wee to the pros.

1960 until 1988. Under his guidance, the team rose from a winless first season to dominate the NFL. They played in five Super Bowls and won two Super Bowl trophies. Landry told his players, "A winner never stops trying."[38]

Players Above the Pack

Like other experts, coaches know that great players share similar traits. They say an exceptional player has a strong work ethic, which means they complete a task well, do it when they are supposed to, and often give more than is expected to a job. The best players seem to understand naturally that mental preparedness is as important as physical preparedness. A great player is dedicated to the team. Bud Wilkinson (1916–1994) was inducted into the College Football Hall of Fame as a coach in 1969. He said "If a team is to reach its potential, each player must be willing to subordinate his personal goals to the good of the team."[39] A good player realizes that all team members must work for the same goal.

An extraordinary player also pushes himself or herself as far and as hard as possible. Archie Griffen is a former NFL running back and is college football's only two-time Heisman Trophy winner. According to him, "It's not the size of the dog in the fight, but the size of the fight in the dog."[40]

Walter Payton (1954–1999), who played his entire career for Chicago Bears, put it this way. "A lot of fans were drawn to me because they knew that whatever the score was, I was going to run as hard as I could on every play."[41]

EXTRA POINT

20

Number of straight winning seasons the Dallas Cowboys enjoyed under coach Tom Landry

Cocky or Confident?

Psychologists have conducted studies of the personalities of football players at universities. In the studies, football players scored as less fearful and less worried than other students. They all scored higher than other students in group cooperation.

The experts conducting one test found something that surprised them. They expected football players to rank higher than other males of college age in thrill seeking activities. Instead, the football players scored lower. Quarterbacks scored higher than other football players on traits such as leading others, having self-confidence, being ambitious, and being outgoing. Since quarterbacks lead on the field, the experts suggested that it is not surprising that they also lead off the field. Linebackers and wide receivers had the next highest scores for leadership qualities.

According to the scores, linebackers are more sociable than quarterbacks, and running backs show the most sensitivity to others in social situations. Kickers tested had scores showing the most compassion and for being the friendliest.

People often portray football players as more self-centered and egotistical than people in other vocations. The studies show that football players have traits that are similar to those of successful people in other lines of work.

Creating Good Luck

Winners in all aspects of life attract people, and football stars draw a huge number of fans. Some fans have deep emotional ties to a certain football team and get upset and depressed when their team loses. There are diehard fans who follow strict customs and traditions before and during every game, as if they are creating a positive vibe for their team. Some of the habits are really more like superstitions. People remember what they were wearing when their team had a big win, and afterwards they must always wear that same outfit while watching a game. Others have clothes they consider lucky because they met a player while wearing them, or they have a sweatshirt or pajamas that bears their team's logo. Some wear lucky underwear, socks, and hats. The lucky clothes might not get cleaned until the season is over, or the owners may never wash them in order to preserve the good luck.

Some supporters must watch each game on the same television set while sitting in the same chair. They do the same victory song and dance an exact way that cannot vary. There is a suspicion in some people's minds that their team does worse when they are not watching, so they go without breaks while the ball is in play. Many fans stand during tense times, not because they are stressed they say, but to help their team pull through. A few fans go overboard and ban certain family members from watching a game with them because something made them think those relatives are bad luck.

Football players at the University of Georgia touch a stone of Uga, the university's bulldog mascot, for good luck as they take the field on game days.

Coaches and players have created just as many traditions and superstitions to follow before a game. Coach Nick Saban traditionally received a penny from his daughter before each Alabama game. One of Saban's players, offensive coordinator Jim McElwain, wrote the names of his five family members on five gum wrappers and tucked them in his pocket before playing. Defensive end Corey Sears, who played for the St. Louis Rams, the Arizona Cardinals, and the Houston Texans, had a tradition of eating a whole lemon before playing.

At the University of Notre Dame, the players all touch a "Play Like a Champion Today" sign as they leave the locker room. At the University of Georgia, team members touch the stone statue of Uga, their mascot. Some teams have a certain meal they eat before each game, and the menu can never change, or things will not be right. Austen Arnaud goes against the old saying that for good luck a person should always dress and undress with the right foot first. He dresses the entire left side of his body first—left foot, pants leg, shirt sleeve, and shoe. Arizona State quarterback Steven Threet honors his grandfather by wearing a T-shirt that belonged to him. The shirt, now raggedy, has been worn under his pads for every game since the middle of high school.

Pink Psychology

Hayden Fry, who coached the Iowa Hawkeyes for twenty years, did something very unusual to help his team. It had more to do with psychology than luck. He had majored in psychology in college and remembered reading that the color pink has a relaxing effect on people. Fry wanted to calm his team's opponents and curb their energy. So he had the locker room for the visiting team painted pink—from top to bottom and all over. Pink lockers, toilets, and showers were even added. Players from opposing teams said it had a strange effect, but they also said it did not bother them. Fry wrote in his book, *A High Porch Picnic*: "When I talk to an opposing coach before a game and he mentions the pink walls, I know I've got him. I can't recall a coach who has stirred up a fuss about the color and then beat us."[42]

Coach Hayden Fry had the idea to decorate the University of Iowa's visitor locker room with pink walls, carpet, and other fixtures under the theory that the color would have a relaxing psychological effect on his team's opponents.

Lucky customs and habits make for fun traditions, but they do not determine success in anything. Players need proper training of the mind and body. They must gain experience and develop their instincts for the game and be willing to push themselves to their limits. Football players, coaches, and fans seem to feel the hard work and hard knocks are worth it. After all, it is football, the game America loves to watch. According to Tom Landry, "Football is an incredible game. Sometimes it's so incredible, it's unbelievable."[43]

Players work their magic on the field. They execute a precise throw or kick a football and send it soaring in a perfect arc to land between the goal posts. They leap and snatch a ball out of the air with their eyes closed. Great football players know that smart playing keeps the laws of physics working with them instead of against them.

NOTES

Chapter 1: The Games Begin

1. Quoted in Craig Townsend. "It's Mind Over Matter." *MindTraining.net*. www.mindtraining.net.
2. Quoted in "10k Truth Football Quotes." www.10ktruth.com.
3. "Famous Quotes by Vince Lombardi." *vincelombardi.com*. www.vincelombardi.com.
4. "Famous Football Quotes." Great Quotes.com. www.great-quotes.com.
5. Quoted in Timothy Gay, Ph.D. "The Steelers Get Lucky." *The Physics of Football*. New York: HarperCollins Publishers, 2005, p. 2.

Chapter 2: Grit for the Gridiron: Training

6. "Famous Football Quotes."
7. Townsend, "It's Mind Over Matter."
8. Interview: Jennifer McKerley with Troy Hatton, Football Strength and Conditioning Coordinator, University of New Mexico. January 14, 2011.
9. Interview with Troy Hatton.
10. Carlos "Big C" Holmes. "Bengals' Palmer Works to Improve Arm Strength," *Dayton Daily News*. Dayton, Ohio: Cox Ohio Publishing, June 26, 2009. www.daytondailynews.com.
11. Interview with Troy Hatton.
12. Interview with Troy Hatton.
13. Interview: Jennifer McKerley with Aaron Wellman, Football Strength and Conditioning Coach, San Diego State University. January 6, 2011.
14. Interview: Jennifer McKerley with Dave Binder, Head Athletics Trainer, University of New Mexico. January 14, 2011.
15. Townsend, "It's Mind Over Matter."

Chapter 3: The Perfect Arc: Passing, Punting, and Kicking

16. Gay, *The Physics of Football*, p. 128.

Chapter 4: Catching and Running

17. Reed Albergotti. "The NFL's Most Exciting Receiver." *The Wall Street Journal*. January 16, 2009. http://online.wsj.com.
18. "10k Truth Football Quotes."

Chapter 5: Blocking and Tackling

19. "Famous Quotes by Vince Lombardi."
20. "Famous Football Quotes."
21. Quoted in Agnieszka Biskup. "Defense," *Football, How it Works (The Science of Sports)*. Mankato, Minnesota: Capstone Press, 2010, p. 21.
22. Quoted in Michael Freeman. *Jim Brown: The Fierce Life of An American Hero*. NY: HarperCollins Publishers, 2006, p. 14.
23. Quoted in "All Famous Quotes, Museum of All the Famous Quotes and Sayings!" www.allfamousquotes.net.

Chapter 6: Staying in the Game: Nutrition, Equipment, and Injuries

24. Interview with Troy Hatton.
25. Interview with Troy Hatton.
26. Interview with Dave Binder.
27. Gay, *The Physics of Football*, p. 61.
28. "10k Truth Football Quotes."
29. "10k Truth Football Quotes."
30. Mike Pereira. "Helmet-to-Helmet Hits March Week 6." *Fox Sports.com*. http://msn.foxsports.com.

Chapter 7: A Winning Mindset: The Psychological Game

31. Quoted in "Johnny Unitas." www.sportsecyclopedia.com.
32. Townsend, "It's Mind Over Matter."
33. "10k Truth Football Quotes."
34. "10k Truth Football Quotes."
35. Townsend, "It's Mind Over Matter."
36. "Famous Quotes by Vince Lombardi."
37. "Famous Quotes by Vince Lombardi."
38. "Tom Landry." *Answers.com*. www.answers.com.
39. Quoted on "Bud Wilkinson." *RivalryFootball.com*. http://webcache.googleusercontent.com.
40. "10k Truth Football Quotes."
41. "10k Truth Football Quotes."
42. Quoted on Tim Hyland. "The Pink Locker Room at Iowa's Kinnick Stadium." *About.com:College Football*. http://collegefootball.about.com.
43. Quoted on Noel Jameson. "12 Tom Landry Quotes to Commemorate the Birthday of a Football Great." *SearchWarp.com*. www.famous-quotes-and-quotations.com.

angular: Concerning the features of a revolving body that are measured in reference to its axis of rotation.

bladder: The inflatable lining of a football or basketball.

cognitive psychologist: A person trained to study mental processes including how people think, understand, remember, solve problems, and learn.

flak jackets: Reinforced sleeveless jackets worn by soldiers and policemen for protection against gunfire or shrapnel.

nutritionists: People trained in the science of the process by which humans take in and utilize food material.

parabola: A u-shaped curve with specific mathematical properties; the exact mathematical curved path that an object in flight follows.

physics: Branch of science concerned with the properties of matter and energy and the relationships between them. It is based on mathematics and traditionally includes mechanics, optics, electricity and magnetism, acoustics, and heat.

pituitary gland: One of the major glands that make up the endocrine system, which releases hormones, like growth hormones, that affect almost every organ and function of the body.

prolate spheroid: A spheroid is a shape produced by rotating an ellipse or oval around one of its axes. Prolate means stretched out. A prolate spheroid is one in which the axis running the length of the shape (polar axis) is greater than the equatorial diameter.

proportional: Can be compared to or corresponds to.

rotator cuff: The set of muscles and tendons that stabilize the shoulder.

scrimmage: Imaginary line on a football field, parallel to the goal lines, on which the ball is placed at the start of a down and on either side of which the offense and defense line up.

static: Characterized by a fixed or stationary condition.

subconscious: That part of the mind operating beneath or beyond the conscious, which is the part of the mind of which the individual is aware.

FOR MORE INFORMATION

Books

Madeline Goodstein. *The Physics of Balls in Motion (Sports Science Projects)*. Berkeley Heights, NJ: Enslow Publishers, Inc., 1999. This book covers the characteristics and motions of the plain rubber ball, as well as those used for baseball, basketball, golf, tennis, and football. It has clear illustrations of the ideas presented and suggestions for fun demonstrations.

Agnieszka Biskup. *Football, How it Works (The Science of Sports)*. Mankato, Minnesota: Capstone Press, 2010. Lots of photos fill this book to illustrate the basic concepts of football, the positions played, and the basic laws of physics involved in the game. It has many information boxes filled with interesting facts.

David J. Miller. *The Super Book of Football*. Boston: Little, Brown and Company, 1990. Filled with photos, this book covers football from its beginnings, how the game evolved, the basics of the game and its positions, the greatest plays, the greatest players, and all about the NFL. It also has record lists and timelines.

George Sullivan. *Power Football*. NY: Atheneum Books for Young Readers, 2001. All the outstanding running backs of the twentieth century and their greatest plays are featured.

Mark Stewart and Mile Kennedy. *Touchdown, the Power and Precision of Football's Perfect Play*. Minneapolis: Millbrook Press, 2010. With photos of players in action, this book tells about the history and art of the touchdown, the ten that are the most unforgettable, as well as fumbles, great goofs, and more.

Internet Sources

Wilson. "Making an NFL Football." www.wilson.com/en-us/football/news/88696/. This site gives an inside look of the Wilson factory that makes the Official NFL Game Ball. It shows how Wilson workers in Ada, Ohio, make thousands of NFL Game Balls each year by hand from genuine leather hides.

Popular Mechanics. "Football Physics: The Anatomy of a Hit." www.popularmechanics.com/outdoors/sports/physics/4212171. This site reports on what happens when a bone-jarring tackle takes a player down: the physics involved, the injuries, the g-forces, and how gear protects.

Sports Fitness Advisor. "Strength Training for Football." www.sport-fitness-advisor.com/strength-training-for-football.html. This site offers extensive guidelines for training and conditioning for many sports. It covers strength training, endurance training, nutrition, and much more.

The Physics Classroom. "Momentum and Its Conservation." www.physicsclassroom.com/class/momentum/u4l1b.cfm. Many tutorials in all areas of physics are offered on this site. It covers the physics of football plays and impacts in simple terms and has many diagrams and drawings to help students understand.

INDEX

Lombardi trophy, 19, *19*
Luck, 91–94

M
Madden, John, 22–23
Magnus effect, 44–45
Mass, center of, 67
McElwain, Jim, 93
McGill rules, 14–15
Mental traits of successful players, 85–89, 90–91
Momentum, 58–60, *59*, 62, 63–64
Montana, Joe, 21
Motion, laws of, 36–39, 66–67
Mouth guards, 78
Movies, 11–12, *12*
Muscles
    building, 24–25, *25*
    fibers, 30–31
    flexibility, 32–33
    imbalance, 33
    nutrition, 71–72
    physiology, *23*, 23–24
    strength training, 26, *27*, 28–29
    strengthening through thought, 26

N
Namath, Joe, 10, *86*, 87
National Collegiate Athletic Association
    (NCAA), 21
National Football Conference (NFC), 19
National Football League (NFL)
    banned substances, 73–75
    conferences, 19
    Fantasy Football, 13
    helmet-to-helmet hits, 83
    history, 18
    Super Bowl viewership, 10
Newton, Isaac, 37, *37*
Newton's laws of motion, 36–39
Numbers, uniform, 36
Nutrition, 68–73, *70*, 75

O
O'Brien, Chris, 18

P
Pads, shoulder and body, *77*, 79
Palmer, Carson, 28–29
Parcells, Bill, 33
Passing. *See* Throwing the football
Payton, Walter, 91
Personality traits, 85–89, 90–91
Physics
    collision, 62–64
    force of collisions, 64–66
    gripping the football, 56–57
    kicking the football, 39, *40*, 41–42
    momentum, 58–60, *59*
    throwing the football, 36–39, 42–45
    torque in tackling, 66–67
Physiology, *23*, 23–24
Popular culture, 11–13
Popularity, 10–11, 20
Porter, Jerry, 25
Princeton University, 13–14
Professional football history, 17–20
    See also National Football League (NFL)
Projectile motion, 39, 43
Protective equipment, 76–79, *77*
Protein intake, 71
Psychology
    coaching, 89–90
    mental traits of successful players, 85–87,
        90–91
    strengthening muscles through thought, 26
    zoning in or out, 87–89

Q
Quarterbacks
    throwing the football, 42–45, *43*
    training, 28–29
Quiet eye method, 48–49

R
Random drug testing, 75
Receivers, 46–52, *48*, *51*
Reeves, Joseph Mason, 76
Resistance training, 26, *27*, 28–29
Rockne, Knute, 21

PICTURE CREDITS

ABOUT THE AUTHOR

Jennifer McKerley is the author of fiction and nonfiction books for children, including *Goblins*, *The Kraken*, *Hydra*, *Swamp Monsters*, and *Egyptian Mythology*. She enjoys living in New Mexico. You can visit her website at www.jenniferguessmckerley.com.